Cambridge Elements

Elements in Women in Music
edited by
Rhiannon Mathias
Bangor University

MUSIC AT A FLORENTINE CONVENT

The Biffoli-Sostegni Manuscript and Suor Maria Celeste Galilei

Laurie Stras
University of Southampton

Shaftesbury Road, Cambridge CB2 8EA, United Kingdom

One Liberty Plaza, 20th Floor, New York, NY 10006, USA

477 Williamstown Road, Port Melbourne, VIC 3207, Australia

314–321, 3rd Floor, Plot 3, Splendor Forum, Jasola District Centre, New Delhi – 110025, India

103 Penang Road, #05–06/07, Visioncrest Commercial, Singapore 238467

Cambridge University Press is part of Cambridge University Press & Assessment, a department of the University of Cambridge.

We share the University's mission to contribute to society through the pursuit of education, learning and research at the highest international levels of excellence.

www.cambridge.org
Information on this title: www.cambridge.org/9781009598644

DOI: 10.1017/9781009387125

© Laurie Stras 2025

This publication is in copyright. Subject to statutory exception and to the provisions of relevant collective licensing agreements, no reproduction of any part may take place without the written permission of Cambridge University Press & Assessment.

When citing this work, please include a reference to the DOI 10.1017/9781009387125

First published 2025

A catalogue record for this publication is available from the British Library

ISBN 978-1-009-59864-4 Hardback
ISBN 978-1-009-38711-8 Paperback
ISSN 2633-6871 (online)
ISSN 2633-6863 (print)

Additional resources for this publication at www.cambridge.org/stras

Cambridge University Press & Assessment has no responsibility for the persistence or accuracy of URLs for external or third-party internet websites referred to in this publication and does not guarantee that any content on such websites is, or will remain, accurate or appropriate.

For EU product safety concerns, contact us at Calle de José Abascal, 56, 1°, 28003 Madrid, Spain, or email eugpsr@cambridge.org

Music at a Florentine Convent

The Biffoli-Sostegni Manuscript and Suor Maria Celeste Galilei

Elements in Women in Music

DOI: 10.1017/9781009387125
First published online: December 2025

Laurie Stras
University of Southampton
Author for correspondence: Laurie Stras, l.a.stras@soton.ac.uk

Abstract: The Biffoli-Sostegni manuscript, MS 27766 of the Bibliothèque du Conservatoire royal de Bruxelles, is the only volume of sixteenth-century polyphony with a secure provenance in a female convent. Its extraordinary survival is made all the more important by its origin at the Florentine convent of San Matteo in Arcetri, the convent in which Suor Maria Celeste Galilei, daughter of Galileo Galilei, spent the last two-thirds of her life. This Element uses archival sources related to San Matteo to create a historical context for the manuscript's music and the lives of the nuns for whom it was written. Analysis of the music is accompanied by both notated and audiovisual musical examples, performed by the UK all-female early music ensemble, Musica Secreta.

This Element also has a video abstract: www.cambridge.org/EWIM_Stras_abstract

Keywords: Suor Maria Celeste Galilei and music, Renaissance convents, Renaissance music manuscripts, Renaissance nuns and music, Renaissance music in Florence

© Laurie Stras 2025

ISBNs: 9781009598644 (HB), 9781009387118 (PB), 9781009387125 (OC)
ISSNs: 2633-6871 (online), 2633-6863 (print)

Contents

1 Introduction   1

2 Historical Context for the Biffoli-Sostegni Manuscript   7

3 Sound and Music in the Life of the Convent   27

4 The Music of the Biffoli-Sostegni Manuscript   37

5 Conclusion   74

   Appendix A: Manuscript Contents   76

   Appendix B: The Women of San Matteo   83

   References   95

Music at a Florentine Convent

The Biffoli-Sostegni Manuscript and Suor Maria Celeste Galilei

Elements in Women in Music

DOI: 10.1017/9781009387125
First published online: December 2025

Laurie Stras
University of Southampton
Author for correspondence: Laurie Stras, l.a.stras@soton.ac.uk

Abstract: The Biffoli-Sostegni manuscript, MS 27766 of the Bibliothèque du Conservatoire royal de Bruxelles, is the only volume of sixteenth-century polyphony with a secure provenance in a female convent. Its extraordinary survival is made all the more important by its origin at the Florentine convent of San Matteo in Arcetri, the convent in which Suor Maria Celeste Galilei, daughter of Galileo Galilei, spent the last two-thirds of her life. This Element uses archival sources related to San Matteo to create a historical context for the manuscript's music and the lives of the nuns for whom it was written. Analysis of the music is accompanied by both notated and audiovisual musical examples, performed by the UK all-female early music ensemble, Musica Secreta.

This Element also has a video abstract: www.cambridge.org/EWIM_Stras_abstract

Keywords: Suor Maria Celeste Galilei and music, Renaissance convents, Renaissance music manuscripts, Renaissance nuns and music, Renaissance music in Florence

© Laurie Stras 2025

ISBNs: 9781009598644 (HB), 9781009387118 (PB), 9781009387125 (OC)
ISSNs: 2633-6871 (online), 2633-6863 (print)

Contents

1 Introduction — 1

2 Historical Context for the Biffoli-Sostegni Manuscript — 7

3 Sound and Music in the Life of the Convent — 27

4 The Music of the Biffoli-Sostegni Manuscript — 37

5 Conclusion — 74

Appendix A: Manuscript Contents — 76

Appendix B: The Women of San Matteo — 83

References — 95

1 Introduction

This Element is inspired by a book: the Biffoli-Sostegni manuscript, MS 27766 of the Bibliothèque du Conservatoire royal de Bruxelles, a fragile but not insubstantial manuscript of music that was acquired in the early years of the twentieth century. Nothing is known of its whereabouts in the nineteenth century. Perhaps it changed hands more than once, circulating in private collections before it was purchased by the library. Nonetheless, we can be certain that it was created in Florence in the sixteenth century; it may have remained there until the early 1800s, when Napoleon's authorities abolished almost all of Italy's convents and confiscated their property.

The possessions of Renaissance religious institutions still in existence today are always precious, since so much has been lost or destroyed. Yet the Biffoli-Sostegni manuscript is even more special, since it is the only surviving volume of sixteenth-century polyphony that verifiably began its life in a convent. There are fewer than two dozen manuscripts of convent polyphony remaining from before the beginning of the sixteenth century, mostly from the fifteenth century; and about the same number of prints associated with nuns, mostly from the last quarter of the sixteenth century (Yardley 1986, 26–27; Stras 2017a, 196–97).

This scarcity of material makes any source consequential, but it also brings with it the danger of moving from the specific to the general: while it is possible to mine the manuscript for every scrap of information, what it tells us may be more relevant to the musical culture of its original institution than it is to sixteenth-century convent music in the wider sense. But at the very least, the manuscript becomes a proof of concept – that even a modest convent outside of a city centre could have a rich musical life.

1.1 The Manuscript and Its Origins

The Biffoli-Sostegni manuscript is bound in leather and copied on ruled and folded *carte reale*, approximately A3 size (420 mm x 280 mm). There are 170 leaves in the book, of which 166 have writing on at least one side. The front and back covers both once held an oval medallion, on which was painted a coat of arms (the back medallion is missing). Around each medallion space is embossed a name, in Latin: *Sorori Angiolete de Biffolis* and *Sorori Clementie de Sostegnis* – 'to Suor Agnoleta Biffoli' and 'to Suor Clemenzia Sostegni'. The manuscript is loosely organised into two sections, each beginning with a setting of the Mass Ordinary: sixty-six works in four voices (this section also interpolates a three-voice work), then ten three-voice works. A fragment of a two-voice work is copied on a page left blank by the copyist at the end of the book.[1] The works range in complexity and length, from the strictly homophonic to dense polyphony, including vernacular song, antiphons, responsories, litanies, alternatim psalms and Magnificats for Vespers, and the masses.

The music is written in choirbook format, with beautiful filigree initials – called 'cadels' – at the beginning of each separate piece or section. Male grotesques adorn many cadels, but from a few, nuns' faces peer out, some in the act of singing (Figure 1). Some cadels are decorated further with yellow colour, and on a single page, a larger pen and colour drawing depicts the women's coats of arms hanging in an olive tree (Figure 2). Many cadels contain tiny inscriptions that both celebrate the nuns and give us further clues about the book's genesis: the date 1560, and the principal copyist's name, Antonius Morus – a Latinised form of Antonio Mori, or Moro.[2]

Most of the music is anonymous, with only three composers' names attached to a handful of works – Moro himself, Francesco Bocchini, and Adriano Willaert. As beautiful as the manuscript is, however, its materials have not easily stood the test of time: the acid in the iron gall ink has eaten away the paper in many places, leaving patches of some pages disintegrating into dust.[3] This damage has meant that, for the purposes of musicological study and performance, many of the pieces have needed reconstruction, ranging from single notes to extended passages in

Figure 1 B-Bc MS 27766, 64v: *Verbum caro factum est*, Tenor, singing nun (Bibliothèque du Conservatoire royal de Bruxelles).

---

[1] See Appendix A, Manuscript Contents.

[2] Musicological literature unanimously refers to Antonius Morus as Antonio Moro; however, the plural form of his family name, Mori, is by far more common in mid sixteenth-century Florence; see datasets provided by the DECIMA project, https://decima-map.net. A Suor Antonia di Niccolò Mori was present at San Matteo between 1545 and 1583.

[3] The manuscript has been in conservation now since the 2010s and is not available for public consultation, so this Element has been written with the aid of high-resolution colour and black-and-white photographs.

Figure 2 B-Bc MS 27766, 23v: the Biffoli and Sostegni coats of arms (Bibliothèque du Conservatoire royal de Bruxelles).

multiple parts: in the music examples, editorial reconstruction is indicated by vertical square brackets.

The manuscript is not a new discovery: nearly 100 years ago, Charles van den Borren, librarian of the Brussels Conservatoire, noticed the names of the two nuns on its binding and surmised that it came from a Florentine convent (van den Borren 1934, 23–26). In 1996, the Italian musicologist Lucia Boscolo published a detailed codicological study, together with an expanded inventory identifying liturgical usage and concordances (Boscolo 1996).[4] British scholar Iain Fenlon and American scholar James Haar identified that the copyist, Antonio Moro, had also produced a handful of other important sources of early sixteenth-century secular and sacred music (Fenlon and Haar 1988, 127).

I began looking at the Biffoli-Sostegni manuscript in 2015, when I was trying to understand the musical context for another group of works I felt sure had been composed for nuns (Stras 2017a; 2017b; 2018). The names of the two nuns on the binding are from Florentine families, and the set of antiphons for St Clare convinced everyone who had written about the book that it was prepared for a convent of Poor Clares – the second, female order of the Franciscans. However, no further work had been done to establish which Florentine Clarissan convent was home to Suor Agnoleta and Suor Clemenzia.

Close to the beginning of the manuscript, the copyist placed music that suggested the convent could be dedicated to an Apostle: a hymn for the feasts of the Apostles and the Vespers psalms for the Common of Saints. Only two Clarissan convents in Florence fit this description: the rich San Jacopo in via Ghibbelina, right in the centre of town, and the less prestigious San Matteo in Arcetri, which was some distance outside the city. Close to the end of the manuscript, however, is a setting of the Gospel reading for the Feast of St Matthew, which is a rather more substantial clue, as convents would have wanted dedicated music to use for their patronal feast. And indeed, in 2020 I found both Suor Clemenzia and Suor Agnoleta in what remains of San Matteo's papers. Having identified the manuscript's origins, I could use other materials preserved in other archives to learn who Suor Agnoleta and Suor Clemenzia were, to understand the world in which they lived, and to place their music in a much clearer context.

The manuscript's connection to San Matteo also links it to one of the convent's, and Florence's, most famous nuns, Suor Maria Celeste Galilei, the eldest daughter of Galileo Galilei. Although Galileo was a scientist, most of his family, including Suor Maria Celeste, were musicians. From the time she

---

[4] Boscolo and Giulio Cattin also produced two much shorter studies on specific pieces in the manuscript (Boscolo 2002; Cattin 2003).

entered San Matteo in 1612, Suor Maria Celeste would have been part of the convent's musical forces, and towards the end of her life she was responsible for the choir. The music of the Biffoli-Sostegni manuscript provides more insight into Suor Maria Celeste's daily existence and the few references to music in the letters she wrote to her father.

While the manuscript's historical implications are fascinating in themselves, its contents are also hugely important to the understanding of women's music-making at the end of the European Renaissance. The works relate to a full range of musical events, from everyday prayers and hymns to the most solemn of the convent's feasts. There is also a wide range of compositional styles and performance requirements, from very simple harmonisations suitable for people with only the most basic training, to complex polyphony only within the reach of virtuoso singers. The manuscript is clearly dated 1560, but some of the works were composed decades earlier, perhaps even in the fifteenth century. All are for either three or four equal voices, that is, to be sung by a single-sex ensemble of equal maturity, and many appear to have been composed specifically for nuns – perhaps even for (or by) the nuns of San Matteo.

1.2 The Other Primary Sources

The archive of San Matteo in Arcetri is now held by the Archivio di Stato in Florence. It is not large and consists mostly of documents relating to legal disputes from the seventeenth and eighteenth centuries, and the dissolution of the convent by the Napoleonic authorities in 1808. One of the two remaining bundles of exclusively sixteenth-century documents was irretrievably damaged by the disastrous flood of the Arno in 1966. However, the other, a large vellum-bound volume with the word *Ricordanze* embellished on its cover, is well preserved.[5] It contains *ricordi* (or memos) of major financial transactions dating from as early as 1519, with a more organised, itemised ledger beginning in 1530 and ending in 1563. There are further random entries dated into the 1570s, as if the scribe had run out of space elsewhere and just needed a place to preserve some notes.

The *Ricordanze* contains details of the convent's household income and expenses, recorded by the convent's chamberlains (*camerlinghe*). Crucially, this includes the names of girls entering the convent as choir nuns (*monache*), servant nuns (*serviglie*), and boarders (*in serbanza*).[6] These entries contain

---

[5] Archivio di Stato Firenze (I-Fas), Corporazioni religiose sopresse dal governo francese (CRSGF) 6 – San Matteo, *pezzo* 35; hereafter the *Ricordanze*.

[6] The terms *per serviglia* and *in serbanza* (or *serbo*) are linguistically related but generally mean different things in sixteenth-century convents. *Serviglia* suggests servitude, but accepting a girl *in serbo* can also mean that she was to be placed in the convent for education, as an *educanda* (Strocchia 2003).

information about the date and, the girl's family – generally the name of the parent, grandparent, uncle, or aunt placing her in the convent and making her dowry payment. Sometimes, additional payments were made for the girl to have a *maestra* – a nun who provided for her spiritual and pastoral needs, as well as her education – or for the clothing ceremony, or vestition, in which she received the habit (and perhaps a new name) and took the vows of a novice, and by which she officially moved from her secular to her religious family.

The *Ricordanze* also provides a vivid record of the expenses for feast days, and for the convent's testatory obligations: prayers, masses, and other devotions said on behalf of individuals who had given money or property to the convent, normally in their wills, to ensure their souls' swift passage through purgatory and on to Heaven after death. A much later *Sbozzo degli Obblighi* (literally, Sketch of Obligations) compiled in 1694 gives details of all the obligations still celebrated by the convent, some of which were established in the fifteenth century.[7] It serves as a useful cross-reference to some of the entries in the *Ricordanze*, as well as proof that the nuns were still musically active into the late seventeenth century.

Apart from these two separately bound sources, the records of the *Deputati sopra i monasteri* and loose bundles of legal documents from San Matteo, also housed in the Archivio di Stato, have helped me to understand the chronology of some of the nuns at the convent. The records of sixteenth- and early seventeenth-century convents' admissions, professions (the solemnisation of a nun's vows), and visitations (diocesan inspections) in the Archivio Arcivescovile in Florence are far from complete, but still provide essential information. Various writings by Alessandro de' Medici, who was Archbishop of Florence between 1574 and 1605, outline the ever more constricting rules for convent life and worship; these include both loose memos and his 1601 *Trattato sopra il governo dei monasteri*, distributed in manuscript, which formed the practical and ideological basis for many subsequent restrictions on Florence's convents.[8]

The letters of Suor Maria Celeste Galilei, which span the years between 1623 and her death in 1634, provide detail and context. They exist in various different editions, both Italian and English, as well as digital photographs in an online resource hosted by the Museo Galileo.[9] The latest source I have used is San

---

[7] I-Fas, CRSGF 6, *pezzo* 48; hereafter the *Sbozzo*.

[8] Biblioteca Apostolica Vaticana, MS Vat.lat.10444, 333r-348r, *Trattato sopra il governo dei monasteri fatto dal cardinale di firenze per il suo vicario generale l'anno MDCi*; hereafter the *Trattato*. Another copy is in the Biblioteca Nazionale Centrale Firenze (I-Fn), MS Gino Capponi, CIV.

[9] Citations in this Element will be from *Le opere di Galileo Galilei – edizione nazionale*, edited by Antonio Favaro, 20 vols. (1890–1909). Other commercial transcriptions and translation are available; see, for instance, (S. M. C. Galilei 1983; 2000; 2001). The Museo Galileo resource contains both images and transcriptions: https://galileoteca.museogalileo.it/GalManus/?lang=en.

Matteo's *Constituzioni*, newly printed in 1713; while this version introduces a seventeenth-century theological concept, the nun's individual Guardian Angel, that would not have been familiar to Suor Agnoleta and Suor Clemenzia, it outlines rules and behaviours consistent with similar sixteenth-century constitutions (Francescani 1713).

Many of the convent's sources have a memorialising function, both in terms of preserving information and stimulating the memory of people and events. The liturgy works like this, too: not only does the Divine Office repeat daily and weekly, and the whole liturgical cycle return annually, but also the chant melodies and reciting tones are shared, repeated, transformed, so that the nuns' singing bodies and minds were constantly stimulated by a musical and textual resonance. Sound and memory are constants in religious discipline. With sources spanning over 200 years, any unified concept of daily life at the convent is bound to be wildly conjectural, but I am reminded of the time I spent at the convent of Poor Clares in Arundel in the 2010s, to which I retreated once a month to write my book on women and music in sixteenth-century Ferrara. So much seemed familiar from my sixteenth-century sources. While the hours of the Divine Office now happen at different times of the day, they are still manifested by voices and instruments. When sitting in an external parlour, I could sometimes hear a single nun practising her singing. The sisters still play games of their own devising at community celebrations; they still put on dramatisations of saints' lives for their most important feasts. There is still a Great Silence, and there is still an Angelus bell.

2 Historical Context for the Biffoli-Sostegni Manuscript

The ex-convent of San Matteo, once governed by the Franciscan rule of St Clare, sits in the hills of Arcetri about a mile south of the medieval walls of Florence. Only the church exterior and a small courtyard remain of the original buildings. It is hard to overemphasise the bucolic peace of the landscape, barely a forty-five-minute walk from the busy city centre. For centuries, the area has been known for its Verdea wine, produced in the vineyards once worked by the convent. In the 1980s, the historian Giovanni Spadolini said: 'It is a hill that has remained more or less as it was in the fifteenth and sixteenth centuries. With the same cramped and impassable streets: it is impossible to move forward, in two senses. ... A place dear to youthful amazement and enchantment' (Spadolini 1984, 140).

In the sixteenth century, Arcetri provided several important Florentine families with a place of repose, and an opportunity to indulge cultural pursuits.[10] In

---

[10] Benedetto Varchi named villas owned by the Della Luna, the Barducci, the Neri, the Giuccardini, the Lanfredini, and the Benivieni (Varchi 1721, 255). The Villa Buonaccorsi was on the road to Arcetri; there are Buonaccorsi nuns at San Matteo throughout the recorded period. The Villa del

1565, the composer Giovanni Animuccia dedicated a book of madrigals to two sons of the Neri family, suggesting the boys could sing through them while escaping the heat of the summer city: 'When you are, in this hot season, either wearied by more serious study or exhausted by more tiring activities, or when you are truly transported to that Paradise of Arcetri, [these works] will give you some relaxation' (Animuccia 1565, Aii).[11] In the same year, the Villa del Poggio Baroncelli, half a mile from San Matteo, was given by Cosimo I de' Medici to his daughter Isabella de' Medici Orsini, an accomplished musician and patron of the composer Maddalena Casulana, and it soon became her favoured residence and a hub of creative activity.

The Biffoli-Sostegni manuscript shows that these echoes of secular music-making in Arcetri of the mid sixteenth century were complemented by the sound of women singing chant and polyphony behind the enclosed walls of San Matteo. Suor Clemenzia and Suor Agnoleta arrived at the convent at a time when it was undergoing renewal and expansion in the 1540s, as Florence itself settled into what would become almost two more centuries of Medici rule. Like many of the choir nuns at their convent, Suor Clemenzia and Suor Agnoleta came from Florentine minor nobility: Suor Clemenzia's father Roberto was a Medicean administrator, and Suor Agnoleta's father Francesco was a merchant. The manuscript does not make clear the relationship between the two women, although an inscription in the decorations, 'ambo felice, C. A. S.' ('both happy, Clemenzia, Agnoleta Sorores') – at the beginning of the hymn of thanksgiving *Te Deum laudamus* – suggests that it was close (Figure 3). Created almost twenty years after Suor Clemenzia's entry, the manuscript may have been a collective gift to the community from the two nuns, one that commemorated their friendship, the convent's mid century prosperity, and its musical identity.[12] Understanding its music requires a brief summary of the convent's history in the decades prior to the manuscript's commission, establishing a context for the works and their potential meanings for the nuns.

2.1 A Decade of Recovery: San Matteo in the 1530s

In late summer 1529, the peace of Arcetri was shattered by the arrival of Spanish and Imperial troops, who set camp all along the southern hills. They began the

---

Poggio Baroncelli, which in the sixteenth century was owned by the Pandolfini and then the Salviati, was confiscated by Cosimo I de' Medici in 1565.

[11] Source Text 1; original texts from primary sources are included in the Supplementary Material provided online. The book contains three-voice madrigals and motets, mostly for high voices.

[12] Nuns and their families might use personal wealth to endow masses, to commission objects for worship, or to contribute to the convent's buildings in a way that did not confer ownership on an individual nun.

Figure 3 B-Bc 27766, 36v: *Te Deum laudamus*, Cantus, 'T' inscription 'Ambo felice, C. A. S.' (Bibliothèque du Conservatoire royal de Bruxelles).

Figure 4 Giorgio Vasari, *The Siege of Florence* (1556–1562), Sala di Clemente VII, Palazzo Vecchio, Florence (public domain).

ten-month long Siege of Florence, which eventually restored the Medici family to power. Giorgio Vasari's painting of the siege, housed in the Palazzo Vecchio, clearly shows San Matteo in the foreground, with troops exercising outside its walls (Figure 4). While some convents closer to the city were destroyed to prevent them providing shelter to enemy troops, San Matteo was merely evacuated to the house of Medici loyalist Bartolomeo Capponi, which had been commandeered by the republicans.[13]

---

[13] I-Fas, CRSGF 6, pezzo 35, from both credit and debit ledgers, 1530: [37] '*Item*: from Bartolomeo Capponi 100 florins and 7 lire, the florins being what we begged for living and to repair the house'; [188] '*Item*: to clean the street in front of the Capponi house where we were in Florence'; [213] '*Item*: to Bartolomeo Capponi for the return of the 100 gold florins and 7 lire, the florins are those begged from him before, and for the principal of the rent when we were in his house during the siege'. Source Text 2.

When the nuns returned to Arcetri at the end of summer 1530, there was significant work to do on the convent estate, cleaning everything, emptying the wells, reroofing properties, and rebuilding boundary walls. But they also had to bury and commemorate their dead: seven nuns, including the abbess Piera dei Giardelli, died of the plague between 16 August and 15 September, probably brought back from their shelter in Florence. The entries for their masses and offices are the first potential indications of music in the convent's *Ricordanze*. In subsequent years, masses are itemised by the name of the deceased nun: here, there are just too many.

In the first eight months after their return, the nuns relied financially on alms from city government, borrowing or begging from donors, a small number of rents, and the sale of a pair of chickens, walnuts and almonds from the remaining trees, and, disturbingly, the mattresses and bedlinen of the dead nuns. Portions of two dowries, for Chiara Rondinelli and Caterina Anselmi, are also recorded, suggesting that these two girls had only recently joined the convent. The expenses to the end of the year (the Florentine new year began on 25 March, the Feast of the Annunciation of the Blessed Virgin Mary) are heavy with the costs of moving, rededicating the church, and repairs across the convent's entire estate, including all the farms, cottages, and commercial buildings, and – of course – the costs of burials and commemorations. The entries for 1531 show some early signs of recovery: the nuns add earnings from the sale of grain and livestock, from unspecified manual labour, and from spinning. And alongside the funeral masses, the nuns begin again to celebrate their most important sacred feasts: the joint celebration of San Lorenzo and Santa Chiara in August 1531, at which the friars – who had come to celebrate Mass – and the nuns are served eggs, cheese, salad, and beans, with a special ounce of pepper; and the following month when the friars return to celebrate the Feast of San Matteo, they extend resources to buy veal.

A sense of continuity emerges from the pages of the *Ricordanze* which, as surely as the liturgy turns and renews through the church year, charts the convent's feast days, greater and lesser, with details of the food and provisions purchased for the nuns, the convent's *famiglia* (the seculars who served the convent), and the friars who came to celebrate Mass. As the decade progresses, and their debts accrued during the siege are paid off, expenses for more feasts appear in the books: New Year at Annunciation; Passion Sunday; Palm Sunday; Maundy Thursday, Easter and its Octave; Pentecost, San Giovanni Battista; San Lorenzo and Santa Chiara (on consecutive days, but Chiara is a double feast); the Assumption; San Matteo; San Francesco; the Immaculate Conception of the Blessed Virgin Mary (hereafter BVM); and Christmas. They note more local and non-liturgical celebrations, such as Berlinghaccio (Maundy Thursday),

Calendimaggio (May Day), and the Corpus Christi procession of the Compagnia della Santa Annunziata from San Felice.

The orderly progression of the *Ricordanze* is also reflected in the way obligations recur, notably an *ufficio dei morti* and masses on the Feast of San Matteo for the soul of one Corsino Amidei, that was established as early as 1318 (Repetti 1845, 163). However, when the Duke of Florence, Cosimo I de' Medici, introduced a new governance structure for the city's convents in 1545, the *Ricordanze* underwent a major change: significantly, it no longer recorded external income to the convent for obligations and payments for the celebrant friars. Presumably, the new rules meant the *Ricordanze* became one of several accounting books, now recording only household expenses, and that income and expenses derived from external liturgical duties were subsequently kept by the sacristy. Nevertheless, the expenses for feeding the friars are still noted. Moreover, any income and expenses incurred from within the community remain in the *Ricordanze*, so it is possible to track both new entrants and exits (i.e. deaths), as well as any obligations created by the nuns themselves, such as the masses for the plague nuns, for a Suor Arcangiola de Bartoli (d. 1536) and a Suor Angioletta dei Soldini (d. 1548). The obligation for Suor Arcangiola in 1551 includes the *Ricordanze*'s only clear payment to a musician, one 'Bartolomeo sonatore', probably an organist.[14]

Obligations were not just endowed for the dead. On 16 March 1541, the bell-gable of San Matteo's church was struck by lightning.[15] Lighting strikes were common and often deadly, as happened in November 1506, when two nuns in Santa Caterina were killed (Landucci 1883, 279). In gratitude that no one was injured nor extensive damage sustained, the abbess Suor Dianora de Parigi endowed in perpetuity a Mass of the Immaculate Conception, to be sung annually with the participation of six *fratini* (boy novices) and their *maestro*.[16]

> Around dinner time when the lighting hit the bell-gable and by the grace of God we survived with our persons and goods, the reverend mother abbess and the whole convent have in their heart to have celebrated every year on the day mentioned above a mass of the conception with six [boy] novices and their master, and to feed the said novices.[17]

---

[14] I-Fas, CRSGF 6, pezzo 35, [363].

[15] The *Ricordanze* gives the date as 16 March 1640 according to the Florentine calendar. All dates hereafter will be standardised to the Roman calendar, which starts the year on 1 January.

[16] In 1466, after a flood of the Arno, the abbess of another Florentine convent, Le Murate, established a weekly Mass of the Immaculate Conception on Saturdays, to protect the convent from further damage (Lowe 2003, 273).

[17] I-Fas, CRSGF 6, pezzo 35, [254]; Source Text 3. With thanks to Giulio Ongaro for his help with this passage.

In the records for every subsequent year in the *Ricordanze*, the event is referred to as the 'messa de' novizii' or the 'messa de' fratini', with notes of both income of alms specifically for the Mass and the additional expenses of feeding the novices and paying the celebrant.

The 1694 *Sbozzo* confirms that a Mass of the Immaculate Conception was still being celebrated on the anniversary of the strike, but there is no longer any mention of boys:

> The Reverend Sisters of San Matteo in Arcetri must every year, on 16 March, unless this is a Sunday, in which case it should be the following Monday, have sung in their church the Mass of the Immaculate Conception of the Virgin Mary, and this for the vow made by the same, since on 16 March 1540, on which day at the seventeenth hour when the Benediction had been made, the nuns were at table, lightning struck their bell-gable, and by the grace of God no harm was done to any person or any goods, and this is the origin and the cause why, every year at the stated time, for thanks and the preservation in the future from similar perils, the said Mass must be sung, by loose memoranda seen, and by the word of the same reverend mothers.
>
> A Mass of the Immaculate Conception of the Virgin Mary, every year on the day 16 March, unless it is a Sunday, in which case the next Monday.[18]

The provision for boys is unusual: Suor Dianora may have felt her choir was not sufficiently grand, or she may have needed additional vocal forces for the Mass, since numbers at the convent were still so depleted after the plague. The 1478 census shows that San Matteo housed thirty-two '*bocche*' (mouths to feed) (Strocchia 2009, 21), but in 1535, there were only sixteen choir nuns and eight novices, twenty-four in total.[19] By 1540, their number had increased to twenty-eight: there were three recorded deaths, but seven more girls had joined the convent and some of the 1535 novices had surely professed to become choir nuns. This would seem a large enough number from which produce an adequate choir, but the old and infirm were excused from choral duties, and the youngest may not have been ready to join in polyphony. It took another five years for the convent to return to its 1478 capacity: in 1545, there were thirty-one choir nuns and a single novice.[20]

---

[18] I-Fas, CRSGF, 6, pezzo 48, 9; Source Text 4.

[19] Sixteen nuns are named on a contract dated 1535: I-Fas, CSRGF 6, pezzo 44, s.f. See also Appendix B, The Women of San Matteo, a prosopography derived from all the document sources consulted in this study.

[20] Thirty-one nuns are named on a list dated 1545 found in the papers of the *Deputati sopra i monasteri*; I-Fas Auditore dei benefici ecclesiastici e Segreteria del regio diritto, 4892. Gismonda Richasoli was accepted to be a nun in 1544 and the first instalment of her dowry was paid, but no second instalment is recorded and there are no further references to her in the *Ricordanze*; see Appendix B.

The pressure of work on community members must have been considerable in these years. Each woman would hold a variety of posts during her life. Elected abbesses appointed other officers to help them run the convent: at minimum, a sacristan in charge of the church and its contents; two chamberlains overseeing the estate and household finances; a choir mistress to oversee the singing of the Holy Office; an infirmary mistress; and a novice mistress. In addition, on top of her daily responsibility to the choir, every nun would have contributed to the convent's productivity through skilled collective labour, like spinning, and more individual expertise as apothecaries, scribes, musicians, lace-makers, and so on. The oldest, frailest nuns would chaperone external visits in the parlour. Moreover, young girls who were accepted to become choir nuns were placed with a *maestra*, an older woman who would provide both formal spiritual instruction and pastoral care to her *discepola*.[21] Throughout the 1530s and still into the 1540s, there were fewer experienced nuns to shoulder the heaviest burdens.

In 1545, Cosimo I created the *Deputati sopra i monasteri*, four commissioners who worked directly for the duke, and who appointed trustees to oversee the secular affairs of every convent. Although he overtly left the matter of spiritual government of the convents to archbishops, friars, and diocesan officials, his commissioners and the trustees oversaw all finances, estates, and secular employees, in effect removing absolute agency from the abbess. Trustees were also supposed to ensure that convents did not become overcrowded: in San Matteo's case, the recruitment of new nuns had to be balanced with the acquisition or construction of new convent buildings.

Nonetheless, after the struggle of the 1530s, by the mid 1540s San Matteo's financial position had stabilised. It produced wine and textiles, collected rents from its portfolio of shops and farms, and sent grain to the mill it owned with a consortium of other institutions. The convent's burgeoning prosperity up to the conclusion of the Council of Trent in 1563 (when the *Ricordanze*'s regular accounts stop) is shown in several ways: the constant payments for new building work, and the nuns' success in resourcing it through personal donations; the frequency of additional purchases of food for the celebration of feast days – and the quantity and variety of that food; and last, the rapid growth in the number of nuns towards the end of the period. Between 1540 and 1563, there are only seven recorded deaths, but thirty novices are recruited, nine them between 1560 and 1563 alone (more than in the entire decade of the 1540s). By 1563 there are thirty-eight nuns and ten novices, welcoming the priests necessary for sung

---

[21] At least by the seventeenth century, sisters seem to have been placed with the same *maestra*: this was true for both the Galilei sisters and the Squarcialupi sisters (G. Galilei 1904a, 14:39; 1904b, 15:54).

mass almost every month with meats; poultry; cured sausage; cheeses; eggs; artichokes; fennel and other greens; spices such as cinnamon, ginger, and saffron; cherries and figs; and sugar for making *migliacci* (sweet cakes made with pigs' blood). The abundance is particularly noticeable at Carnival and Carnevalino (the period before Advent), contrasting with the more modest fare of eels, dried fish, and kale appropriate for Lent and Advent.

Undoubtedly, the material comforts listed in the accounts are only one side of a more complex story – life in sixteenth-century convents was hard, involving permanent separation from loved ones, hours of manual labour, more hours of singing in the choir, and not a lot of sleep. But this is the world for which the Biffoli-Sostegni manuscript was created in 1560, and it is hard to resist the thought that the musical environment it reveals was also part of the attraction of San Matteo to the families of the nine girls who joined the convent in the subsequent three years.

2.2 Dramatis personæ in the Manuscript

There are very few names in the Biffoli-Sostegni manuscript to which any kind of documentary evidence can be attached. The copyist and composer Antonio Moro, and the donor nuns Suor Clemenzia Sostegni and Suor Agnoleta Biffoli, are the most prominent, but there are also two further composers, Adriano Willaert and Francesco Bocchini, and one other woman, Maddalena, whose names appear.

There is plenty of biographical information available about Adriano Willaert (c. 1490–1562). He was arguably one of the most famous musicians of the first half of the century and was still alive at the time the manuscript was copied, but since his work was so widely available in print, the copyist would not have needed a direct connection to him in order to include his music. Francesco Bocchini is a more obscure figure: he became organist and *maestro di cappella* at the cathedral in Pisa in 1556, and went on to serve in the same capacity as a *cavaliere sacerdote* for the Order of Santo Stefano in Pisa in 1571 (Baggiani 1982, 275–76). Two pieces are attributed to him: *Sancta Maria succurre miseris* (with the name 'Franc.o Bocchino' on 46r) and *In illo tempore: Thomas* (with 'Bocchinus meus F.' on 64r). Although Bocchini is known to have composed many other pieces, these are the only two that survive with his name attached.

Antonio Moro is now best known as the copyist of two other important manuscripts, the Vallicelliana partbooks (I-Rva 35–40) and the 'P.M.' manuscript of Lamentations (I-Fn II.I.285), as well as a single Discantus partbook of madrigals (B-Bc 27731). All his work is associated with Florentine patrons. His earliest sources probably date from the late 1520s or early 1530s; the

Lamentations manuscript was copied in 1559, the year before the Biffoli-Sostegni manuscript. He signals that one motet in the Biffoli-Sostegni manuscript is his own composition (*Sancta Maria succurre miseris*, 41v–43r). Nothing else is known about this mysterious man, whose work has nonetheless contributed so much to our current understanding of Florentine music in the sixteenth century.

On 8 July 1541, Clemenzia Sostegni was accepted to become a nun (*per monaca*) at San Matteo. The *Ricordanze* notes that her father's name is Ruberto and that her dowry of 120 *fiorini* was to be paid in instalments. The first payment included 100 *fiorini* with an additional eight paid to her *maestra*, Suor Caterina Anselmi, for furniture and clothing ('fornimento'). Although the Sostegni had been among Florence's elite for centuries, Suor Clemenzia's immediate family are relatively obscure. A Roberto Sostegni appears briefly in the history of Florence's continued political upheaval: first, in 1537 as a freshly appointed minor official in the civil service of the new duke Cosimo I, and then later that year as the commander of the fortress of the Rocco di Castrocaro, the location of a recent dangerous uprising against Cosimo (Ridolfi 1958, 562; Verna and Zaccaria 2018, 54). It may or may not be a coincidence that the *commissario* of Castrocaro who had suppressed the revolt was Bartolomeo Capponi, in whose house the nuns of San Matteo had sheltered during the siege. Six months later, Maddalena di Giovanni di Ser Piero Sini entered the convent on 20 January 1542. Her dowry of 141 *fiorini* was paid by her grandfather, and she was allocated Suor Antonia Mori as her *maestra*.[22] She was abbess of the convent in the 1590s, serving at least one term just prior to Suor Clemenzia.

On 12 May 1548, Agnoleta Biffoli was accepted *per monaca*, with a dowry of 156 *fiorini*, of which forty were for her furnishings and clothing, and for her 'sacrazione' or profession – an unusual instance of this expense being paid up front, perhaps indicating that she was slightly older than other girls entering the convent, since profession could happen only once a girl had turned sixteen. Her father is named as Francesco; another document in the archive gives her mother's name as Lisabetta.[23] A Francesco di Giovanbattista Biffoli is named in the 1532 Florentine census, living in the quarter of Santa Croce, so this is perhaps her father. When her sister Caterina, who took the name of Suor Cassandra at profession (so as not to confuse her with Suor Caterina

---

[22] The close correspondence between the names of Maddalena's *maestra* and the manuscript's copyist is tantalising, but no evidence can be found to link the two.

[23] I-Fas, CRSGF 6, pezzo 44. s.f. Agnoleta's mother is named in a notarial document dated 8 April 1560, setting out the agreement between the heirs of Francesco Biffoli and the convent for the payment of 150 *scudi d'oro* over three instalments, to be paid from Lisabetta's dowry.

Anselmi), joined the convent the following year, his name is given as Francesco di Giovanbattista Biffoli, *mercciaio*, and his wife's name is given as Maria. It may be that Caterina was much younger than Agnoleta, since she did not profess until 1558.

2.3 San Matteo at the Turn of the 1600s

The household records of the *Ricordanze* stop in 1563, perhaps coincidentally the year of the final session of the Council of Trent. It contains a few sporadic notes, up to 1572, of specific donations towards building costs relating to individual nuns – usually given on the occasion of the nun's profession.[24] There is little in the archives to fill in the history of San Matteo before the turn of the seventeenth century apart from the records of legal disputes. A brief window is opened between 1599 and 1602, during which time Suor Clemenzia was abbess, revealing her struggles to keep the convent financially stable. She was a key witness in a suit against the convent's procurator, who was accused of mismanaging the convent's estate to his own benefit. She also attempted, unsuccessfully, to get permission from the archbishop to sell two unprofitable, flood-prone, and distant farms to raise capital to purchase land from a Florentine magistrate which, she said, would provide all the grain and wine the convent needed. The archbishop's response counselled against selling Church land and buying secular land, which would be subject to a different tax regime.[25]

A more serious conflict between the convent and the diocese emerged in the year between 1600 and 1601. On 22 December 1600, Suor Clemenzia signed a document declaring that San Matteo had the necessary accommodation for girls between the ages of seven and twenty-five to be accepted as boarders (*educanda*), and that they would observe all the rules of enclosed nuns (Figure 5).[26] Taking in boarders, who paid a semester in advance, was becoming a vital part of the convent economy as well as a social need, and many convents across Florence were expanding their communities in this way. Such boarders were allowed to leave the convent, but if they did, they could not return without an additional license. These licenses were difficult to obtain; in 1604, thirteen-year-old Anna Cini applied for permission to re-enter San Matteo after she had left to attend her sister's profession ceremony at another convent; she was refused because her reasons for leaving in the first place were 'nothing but vanity'.[27]

---

[24] The documents retained in the Florentine Archivio di Stato contain another account book from the 1620s to the 1630s: some transcriptions relating to the Galilei women are available in *Le opere de Galileo Galilei*, Vol. 20.

[25] Archivio Arcivescovile Firenze (I-Faav), Atti di monache 5, 21 August 1599.

[26] I-Faav, Atti di monache 6, 22 December 1600.

[27] I-Faav, Atti di monache 9, 24 September 1604.

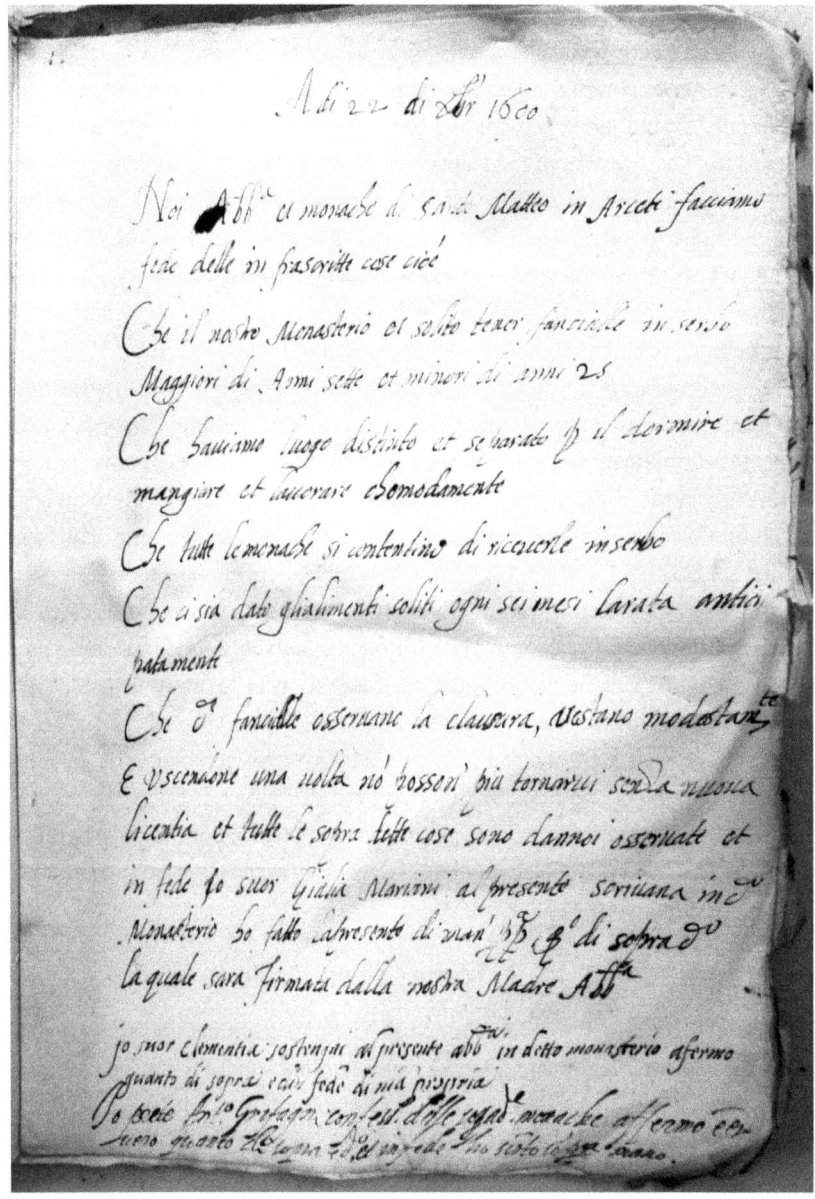

Figure 5 Declaration signed by Suor Clemenzia Sostegni, 22 December 1600 (I-Faav Atti di monache, 6; by permission of the Archivio Storico Arcivescovile di Firenze).

Suor Clemenzia pursued boarder recruitment vigorously, but the diocese soon began to refuse or postpone permission for girls to be admitted as nuns. This mattered because, without this permission, she could not collect dowries. On

13 September 1601 in an application to allow Portia Compagni to profess, Suor Clemenzia reveals what she thinks the reason might be: the diocese was pressuring her to commit the convent's servant nuns to enclosure. She said the community would agree but wanted permission for two older servants to be allowed to enter the church to clean.[28] On 15 September, the Bishop of Pistoia writes to the archbishop, saying that he'd been to the convent and had pleaded with the nuns to yield. Their response was that they had a license from the Grandduchess Giovanna (1547–1578), and that enclosing their servants would cause grave damage to the convent: servant nuns could beg on behalf of the convent, and such alms were regularly recorded in the *Ricordanze*.

On 8 February 1602, the archbishop wrote at the bottom of an application: 'There are many memos relating to these nuns, and we doubt they have the requisite accommodation, and also they are very poor'.[29] More permissions are specifically refused throughout 1602, but finally, on 8 August, the convent's governor Camillo Pandolfini wrote to the archbishop confirming that Suor Clemenzia had held a chapter meeting, and that the professed nuns agreed to enclosing their servant nuns, provided two older servants were allowed to sweep and organise the church. The following day, an application for Maria Guardani, who became Suor Maria Clemenzia, was submitted and it was approved less than two weeks later.

A contract from 1608 shows that Suor Clemenzia was again abbess, and that both Suor Agnoleta and Suor Maddalena were still alive. The next contract in the archive that lists all the professed nuns is dated 1619: Suor Maddalena is still alive (she had been at the convent for seventy-eight years), but Suor Clemenzia and Suor Agnoleta are not.[30]

2.4 Suor Maria Celeste Galilei

When, in 1610, Galileo Galilei returned to Florence from his university post in Padua, he had two illegitimate daughters and an infant son for whom he needed to provide, along with many other familial financial burdens. The toddler Vincenzo stayed with his mother, Marina Gamba; Livia (18 August 1601 – 14 June 1659)

---

[28] A convent's church was a public space, which enclosed nuns were not permitted to enter; see Section 3.2. In the mid seventeenth century, San Matteo appears to have had a high choral gallery rather than an inner choir separated from the outer church by high grates. The biography of Suor Maria Angiola Gini (1631–1664), a nun reputed to have been a living saint who professed at San Matteo in 1647, refers both to a 'Coro in sopra' ('the choir above', p. 143) and the 'scalete del Coro' ('the choir stairs', p. 164). On the other hand, it also refers to 'la grata del Coro' ('the choir grate', p. 102), which may indicate that an older inner choir space still existed (Puliti 1738).

[29] I-Faav, Atti di monache 7, 8 February 1601; Source Text 5.

[30] I-Fas, CRSGF 6, pezzo 44, s.f., 21 April 1619. There are sixty-seven names on the contract, three more nuns than the convent was allowed in 1613, according to a letter from the Cardinal de Joyeuse to the archbishop; I-Faav, Atti di monache 11, 20 January 1613.

travelled with Galileo. Ten-year-old Virginia (13 August 1600 – 2 April 1634) was already in Florence with her grandmother, and she had been offered a place as a boarder at the convent of the Nunziantina at forty-two *scudi* per year, payable six months in advance (G. Galilei 1900, 10:306). Galileo set about looking for a permanent home for both his daughters, but their youth was an obstacle; this much was stressed to him by the Cardinal del Monte in 1611 (G. Galilei 1901, 11:234, 245). While convents could take girls as young as seven as boarders, girls could not be accepted to become a nun until the age of twelve, or profess fully until they were sixteen (Francescani 1596, 318, 321). Perhaps Galileo was looking to save money in the short term since once they were accepted and their dowries paid, he could remove them from his immediate financial obligations. Or perhaps – since he seemed determined to place them together, and the only way to bypass the Florentine diocesan ban on sisters monachising together was to pay a double dowry for the second daughter – he could not afford the superdowry as well as boarding fees.

Eventually Galileo turned to the convent of San Matteo, where his niece Suor Chiara Landucci, daughter of his sister Virginia Landucci, was already a novice.[31] Virginia Galilei was almost twelve years old when her place was secured. A letter dated 11 July 1612, written by the abbess Lodovica Vinta to the archbishop, requests that Virginia, daughter of Galileo Galilei, be permitted to take the place of Suor Clemenzia Sostegni, who must have died very recently (Figure 6).

> My most illustrious, worshipped, and reverend Lord
> With this letter, I come to your most illustrious and reverend lordship, begging you that it might please you to grant a license, so that we may accept into our convent for our professed nun Virginia, daughter of Mr Galileo Galilei, putting her at place number 2, of the blessed memory of Sister Clemenzia Sostegni, observing the orders of the Sacred Congregation, giving the convent the usual dowry and superdowry, and provisions for this girl. And we will remain in perpetual obligation for this grace, to pray to our Lord for all your greatest happiness and exaltation.[32]

Permission was granted the following day and countersigned by the Vicar General on 19 July 1612.

After some negotiation, in November 1613 a license was obtained for both girls to be accepted, so at this point Livia must have joined her sister; however, there was a delay in formalising their entry into religion (G. Galilei 1901,

---

[31] Suor Chiara's secular name had also been Virginia; she is understood to have monachised at some point in 1611.
[32] I-Faav, Atti di monache 11, 11 July 1612; Source Text 6.

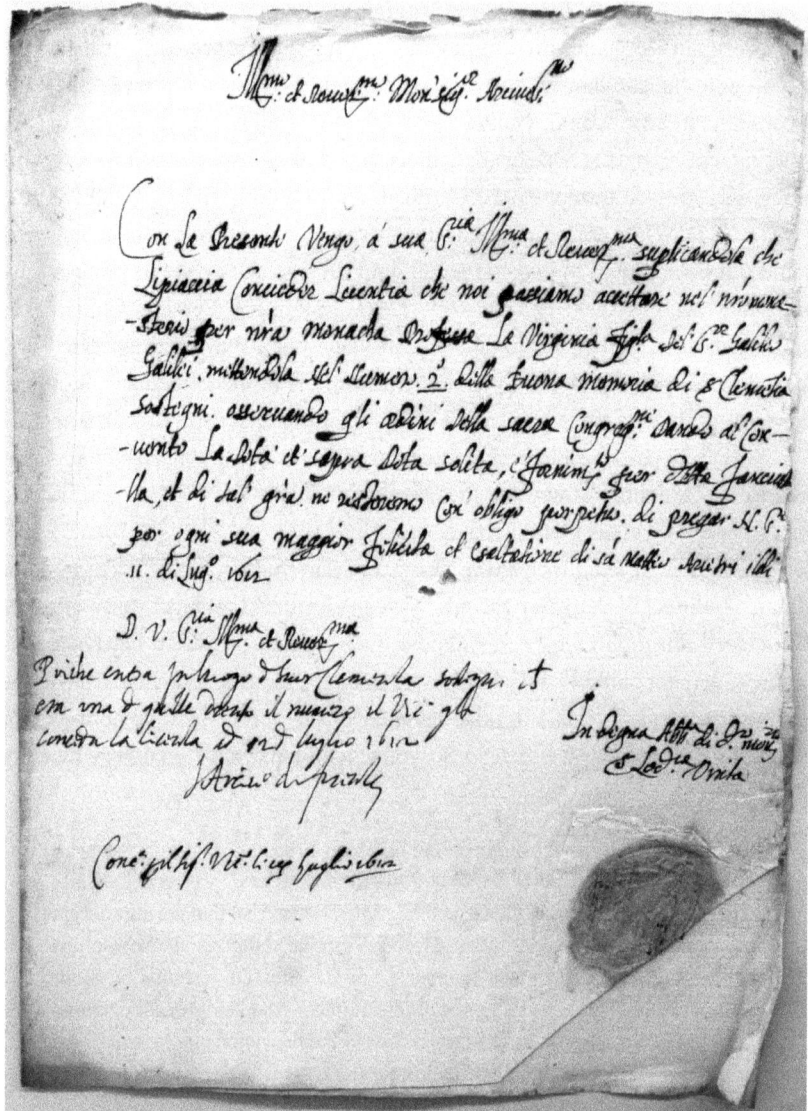

Figure 6 Letter from Suor Lodovica Vinta to Archbishop Alessandro Marzi de' Medici, 11 July 1612 (I-Faav Atti di monache, 11; by permission of the Archivio Storico Arcivescovile di Firenze).

11:588). On 2 July 1614, Suor Lodovica wrote to Galileo, saying that the convent's governor was unhappy that the girls had remained at the convent for so long without becoming novices; the norm between acceptance and vestition was a maximum of four months (Francescani 1596, 319). She said she understood that he had been unwell and that family members were at his home helping out; she proposed that both girls have their ceremonies immediately, while the family were still gathered in Florence (G. Galilei 1902, 12:80–81). Virginia and Livia duly became Suor Maria Celeste and Suor Arcangela, respectively. The next notice of either girl comes when they professed fully at sixteen, Suor Maria Celeste in October 1616, her sister a year later in 1617.

Suor Maria Celeste's correspondence with her father amounts to 123 letters, dated between 1623 and 1633. There are tantalising references to music in them, brief and sometimes cryptic, but nevertheless revealing. Suor Maria Celeste was the granddaughter, niece, sister, and cousin of professional musicians (Vincenzo, Galileo, Michelagnolo, Vincenzo, and Michelagnolo's sons Vincenzo and Alberto); her father was also a skilled musician who played keyboard and lute throughout his life (Fabris 2011). On 22 March 1629, she wrote to her father to ask if he would take back the *chittarone* he had given to her and Suor Arcangela, since it was just gathering dust and she worried it would be damaged every time they were obliged to loan it out (she does not say to whom) (G. Galilei 1904a, 14:27). In exchange, she asked for two breviaries 'since these are the instruments we use every day', recently printed and containing the newest saints' offices, so that they might last for as long as she and her sister might live.

The presence of the *chittarone* is a mystery, but it may have to do with a family prospect that did not materialise. In the summer of 1627, Galileo's brother Michelagnolo corresponded with him over the possibility of Mechilde, Michelagnolo's eldest daughter, joining her cousins at San Matteo. It had been proposed that Suor Maria Celeste would be her *maestra*, and this arrangement seemed to please both young women. Mechilde was sufficiently proficient at the lute to have been offered a place with no dowry in the 'Jesuit' convent in Munich where she was educated, based solely on her musical acumen (G. Galilei 1903, 13:371–72).[33] She had left that convent by the following March and was still exchanging greetings with Suor Maria Celeste in April 1628 (G. Galilei 1903, 13:410). However, shortly after she disappears from the record and her fate is unknown. It may be that the *chittarone* was sent in anticipation of Mechilde's arrival, but since Suor Maria Celeste never received her at San Matteo, the instrument was never used. A few years later, Galileo attempted again to add to the family unit in San Matteo: on 11 March 1631 Suor Maria Celeste wrote that she deeply regretted she could not be *maestra* to yet another Virginia Landucci,

---

[33] Michelagnolo calls Mechilde's school 'the school of certain Jesuit nuns, who recently were brought here from Rome by her Highness'. This must certainly be the institute opened by the exiled English nun Mary Ward in March 1627, where girls were taught the same curriculum as boys, including Latin, languages, and music. The school was suppressed when Ward was imprisoned in 1631, but reopened under the protection of the Elector of Bavaria, Maximilian I.

Galileo's great-niece (G. Galilei 1904a, 14:220–21). The archdiocese had yet again put a restriction on new professions at San Matteo, this time because of its extreme poverty (due, it appears, to unpaid dowries, including her cousin Suor Chiara's).[34] Young Virginia eventually went to the convent of San Girolamo, or San Giorgio di Spirito Santo, alla Costa, another convent with a fine musical institution and a choir that included Margherita Signorini (religious name Suor Placida), daughter of Francesca Caccini (Cusick 2009, 277–79).

On 18 October 1630, Suor Maria Celeste wrote to her father of new responsibilities given to her by the abbess: she had assumed the direction of the choir and organisation of the Divine Office, and she was teaching four young women to sing *canto fermo* (G. Galilei 1904a, 14:156). This would have involved not just the teaching of notation, but also the learning, by memory, of all the psalms and the reciting tones. She said she would enjoy these tasks more if they were not on top of her existing duties and she complained that her poor Latin was a drawback, but tried to see her constant work as a blessing; she noted that it was 'the seventh hour of the night' as she wrote, meaning seven hours after sundown – in late October this would have been well after midnight, as she was preparing for Matins.

The other four direct references to music in Suor Maria Celeste's letters relate to San Matteo's organists and its organ, the only instrument permitted in the convent according to the statutes of the order (Francescani 1596, 53). During Lent 1633, the convent lost the eldest of its three organists, Suor Maria Grazia del Pace, the *maestra* of the Squarcialupi sisters: in February, Suor Maria Celeste wrote that the old nun was very unwell, and to the convent's great grief, she died at the beginning of March. One of the other two organists then appears, with two requests to Galileo regarding music that reveal a desire for closer ties with the secular musical environment in Florence.

Galileo was intimate with the Florentine musical community, with names such as Girolamo Mei, Jacopo Corsi, Francesca Caccini, and Francesco Rasi (Suor Agnoleta Biffoli's step-nephew, see Section 2.5) recurring often in his correspondence. Although he never mentions Vittoria Archilei – the *prima donna assoluta* of Ferdinando I de Medici's court – she and her husband Antonio must have been known to the Galilei family. On 24 July 1612, the week after Suor Maria Celeste's position in the convent was secured, their daughter Maria also secured a place at San Matteo.[35] Suor Maria Eletta, or

---

[34] There were rumours that the young Virginia Landucci was, in fact, another of Galilieo's illegitimate children, and that he had arranged a marriage between her mother, Anna di Cosimo Dieciaiuti, and his nephew to keep Anna close to him. The mystery of young Virginia's birthdate is examined closely in Pagnini (1936).

[35] I-Faav, Atti di monache 11, 24 July 1612.

Madre Archilei, emerges as Suor Maria Celeste's collaborator in organising music for special days of worship.

On 18 June 1633, the week before the Feast of the Nativity of San Giovanni Battista, the city of Florence's patronal feast, Suor Maria Celeste wrote, 'Since where you are there are many excellent masters of music, L'Archilea would like you to obtain something beautiful for her to play on the organ' (G. Galilei 1904b, 15:157). Then, six months later, on 3 December, as the convent was preparing for the Feast of the Immaculate Conception, Suor Maria Celeste's letter demonstrates a more lively and detailed exchange. She enclosed a motet sent by Suor Maria Eletta (either her own composition, or something she copied from the convent's repertoire), and said that, by way of trade, the organist nun would like some sort of instrumental composition (Suor Maria Celeste uses three words interchangeably – 'sinfonia', 'ricercare', and 'sonate'). She specifies further that it needs to be playable in the lower registers, since the organ was missing at least one note at the top, but she doesn't know which (G. Galilei 1904b, 15:342).

Suor Maria Celeste died on 2 April 1634 from dysentery, a relatively common condition in the convent; she often mentioned that either she or another nun was suffering. Her belongings, inasmuch as a nun could own anything, were apparently distributed to her religious sisters, as a later account book notes the sale of a copy of Galileo's book *Il Saggiatore* that had been in the keeping of Suor Maria Celeste's great friend, Suor Luisa Pitti (Pagnini 1936, 62). Suor Maria Eletta survived Suor Maria Celeste by at least ten years; she, too, appears to have received financial support from Galileo. A note in San Matteo's archives, tucked into a file of inventories of the belongings of Cardinal Alessandro Orsini, signed by Vincenzo Galilei and dated 9 May 1644, acknowledges the repayment of twenty-one *lire*, loaned by Galileo to Suor Maria Eletta on 25 September 1641.[36]

San Matteo was outside the city walls, but only half a mile away from the Villa del Poggio Imperiale, as Isabella de' Medici Orsini's 1560s retreat had become. The palace was purchased from the Orsini in 1618, enlarged and remodelled by the Archduchess Maria Maddalena of Austria, and it continued as a locus of female creativity. On 3 February 1625, it was the location for the premiere of Francesca Caccini's *balleto composta in musica*, *La Liberazione di Ruggiero*. A few months later, on 26 May 1625, the Grand Duke heard mass at San Matteo while staying at the Poggio Imperiale (Bonechi 2016, 276). And while, officially, enclosure for the nuns was complete and inviolable, Suor Maria Celeste hints that someone with influence might be able to enter the convent to enjoy the company and recreation: on 12 March 1633, she expresses

---

[36] I-Fas, 6, busta 44, Scritture attenenti alla Casa Orsini, s.f.

surprise and a little concern that the wife of the Tuscan Ambassador to Rome, Caterina Niccolini (Galileo's host during his trial for heresy), was eager to come to San Matteo to watch the nuns perform a *commedia* – in this case, a play on a religious or moral subject (G. Galilei 1904b, 15:66).[37]

2.5 Social and Family Ties

Sixteenth-century nuns maintained and were sustained by social and family structures, some of which they created in the convent themselves, and others that derived naturally from their family relationships outside the convent. The *maestra-discepola* relationship could be strong: Suor Maria Celeste's letters illustrate the bond between her friend Suor Luisa Pitti and her *maestra* Suor Giulia Mariani, 35 years her senior, which involved the younger nun caring for the older one. But close friendships across generations existed outside this formal relationship: Suor Maria Celeste names Suor Luisa and Suor Caterina Angiola Anselmi as her closest friends; Suor Luisa was 17 years older, and Suor Caterina Angiola at least 31 years older than Suor Maria Celeste. These relationships could apparently extend beyond death: when Suor Angioletta de Soldini died in 1548, she left money for masses to be said not only for her own soul, but also that of Suor Arcangiola de Bartoli, who died in 1536.

Naming was another way of creating community. Some girls, for example, Caterina Biffoli, may have been obliged to take a different religious name because the convent already had a nun bearing their first name. The choice might then be a matter of availability. At San Matteo, the name Arcangela belonged to three nuns between 1530 and 1620: the above-mentioned Suor Arcangiola de Bartoli, Suor Arcangela Corsi (secular name Maria, entered 1550), and Suor Arcangela Galilei (secular name Livia, entered 1612). But it also might reflect a desire to honour another nun, or something more personal to the girl herself: Suor Maria Grazia del Pace was born Alessandra, but when she became a nun in 1586 her name was chosen because she was considered 'graziosa e molto amorevole'.[38] Maria Guardini, who entered San Matteo in 1602, was given the name Suor Maria Clemenzia, perhaps to honour Suor Clemenzia Sostegni, who was then the abbess. And of course, Suor Maria Celeste's name honoured her father's preoccupation with the stars.

Family relationships mattered to nuns, both within and outside the convent. Certain families, particularly the Anselmi, the Buonaccorsi, the Gaetani, and the

---

[37] Galileo sent a *commedia* (now lost) to Suor Maria Celeste in October 1633, which she pronounced 'nothing if not wonderful' (G. Galilei 1904b, 15:315).

[38] I-Fn Baldovinetti 87, 'Cose di antichità di casa sua', Ricciardo di Francesco del Pace, 1593, s.f.; Source Text 7. Her sister Maddalena became a nun in San Giuliano and was given the name Maria Anna because she was wise beyond her years ('annosa').

Rondinelli, sent young women into San Matteo throughout the approximately 120 years of records examined for this study, so that aunts and cousins were often together for their lifetimes. But sisters were also commonly placed together, despite tightening restrictions that eventually required families, like the Galilei, to pay additional sums to secure their positions. At San Matteo, this practice actually seems to have increased even as the rules became tighter: between 1530 and 1600 five pairs of sisters join the convent – Biffoli, Canigiani, Santini, Tanini, and Vinta – but between 1600 and 1620, nine pairs are admitted either as boarders or as nuns, or progressing from one state to the other: Anselmi, Canigiani, Filidolfi, Galilei, Giramonti, Mei, Squadrini, Squarcialupi, and Tani.

Outside the convent, trustees were appointed from the nuns' family members, but individually nuns also had to rely on their relations for additional financial support, for which they offered continual prayers in return. Suor Maria Celeste's letters were full of such requests from her to her own father, but his networks were also useful to other nuns; for instance, Suor Polisena Vinta asked for Galilei's help to secure news of her great-nephew and then complained heartily (when he reassured her that said great-nephew was magnanimous in charity) that neither her great-nephew nor his mother had given anything to her (G. Galilei 1904b, 15:247).

Florence was a large, cosmopolitan city, but the closeness of apparently invisible links between families can be surprising. Another Biffoli daughter is intimately connected with the Galilei, in an association that introduces yet another musical element. Gemma di Francesco di Giovannibattista Biffoli could have been around fifteen years younger than Agnoleta, born on 20 April 1549.[39] As a teenager, Gemma married Geri Bocchineri of Prato, with whom she had at least one child, Carlo, born 8 June 1569. Yet she became a widow before she was 30; in late 1579 her brother asked the archbishop for permission for her to enter the convent of the Annalena in Florence.[40] This was granted on 15 January 1580, but only on the condition that she did not 'go in and out' ('purché non entri et esca').

By 1585 Gemma had married again to a minor nobleman from Arezzo, Ascanio Rasi, thereby becoming the stepmother of Francesco Rasi, the singer, composer, and Monteverdi's original Orfeo. One of Gemma and Ascanio's daughters was taught to sing by Giulio Caccini, and became a nun at the convent

---

[39] Archivio storico dell'Opera di Santa Maria del Fiore, Firenze, Registri battesimali, pezzo 230, 131v. While the register refers to Francesco's father as 'giovanfran.co', this is likely an error. Gemma is referred to as 'di Francesco di Giovannibattista' in later documents (G. Galilei 1909, 20:394).

[40] I-Faav, Professioni di monache, pezzo 1 (1577-1582), s.f.; Source Text 8.

of San Salvi (Kirkendale 1993, 560–61). However, family relations gave rise to scandal, when in November 1609, Francesco Rasi began a sexual relationship with the wife of one of Gemma's servants. Francesco then ordered his men to kill both Gemma and the servant, with only Gemma surviving the attack. He was sentenced to death, but he fled to Mantua where he sheltered at the Gonzaga court for ten years.

In autumn 1620, after Gemma's death, Cosimo II de' Medici commuted Rasi's sentence, and the singer returned to Florence (Kirkendale 1993, 594). In what can only be described as a curious turn of events, within a year, Rasi had married Alessandra, the widowed daughter of Carlo Bocchineri – Gemma's granddaughter. Directly after their wedding in in September 1621, the couple returned to Mantua for the marriage celebrations of Eleonora Gonzaga and Emperor Ferdinand II. Rasi died of a sudden illness barely two months later.

Alessandra eventually returned to Tuscany with her third husband, Giovanni Francesco Buonamici, whom she married in 1623; it was through him that she began her friendship with Galileo Galilei. When Alessandra's sister Sestilia married Galileo's son Vincenzo in 1629, the family ties with San Matteo fully intersected: the couple's children were both Gemma's great-grandchildren and Suor Maria Celeste's nephews. It seems likely that Suor Maria Celeste would have known that Sestilia and Alessandra's great-aunts Suor Agnoleta and Suor Cassandra had also lived at San Matteo.

2.6 The Musical Education of Nuns in Early Modern Florence

We might assume Suor Clemenzia and Suor Agnoleta were musically able, but it seems serendipitous that Suor Clemenzia's place at the convent was taken by a young woman who was raised in a musical environment. We know nothing of Suor Maria Celeste's musical education, but she clearly understood music notation and she almost certainly would have had some instrumental tuition.

By the end of the sixteenth century, it was commonplace for girls whose families had sufficient means to be trained in music as a preparation for adult life, whether in a court appointment or – much more frequently – in a convent. In Florence, even the young girls at Santa Caterina, a home for abandoned children, were taught to recite psalms together in regular rhythms (*canto fermo*) (Rombough 2024, 59). Families could be offered dowry reductions or even waivers to entice musical *virtuose*; servant nuns might be elevated to choir status because of their outstanding musical aptitude. One abbess of the Florentine convent at Le Murate used secular women as talent scouts. When offering the services of a poor girl with a 'buon basso' and 'venti voci' – that means, give or take, a three-octave range – her contact said that she would keep the girl in her house to be taught by her musician for a couple of months and then send her on, but if the abbess did not want her, she could be sent back (Stras 2018, 227–28).

While it was common for a girl to receive her musical education prior to entering a convent, secular musicians and priests were engaged to teach nuns more often than might be imagined, even as the Counter-Reformation gathered pace at the end of the sixteenth century: for instance, Ercole Pasquini taught at several convents in Ferrara, Orazio Vecchi in Modena, Vincenzo Pinti in Rome, Antonio Brunelli in Pisa. The circumstances of these lessons might have varied: Pasquini's organ lessons would probably have had to have taken place in the inner convent – for which he was granted a license by the bishop (Stras 2018, 300). Others could have taken place at the grate that separated the nuns from the secular world: there is some evidence from late fifteenth- and early sixteenth-century Florence of a cascading model, in which one nun was taught at the grate, and she was then responsible for passing her knowledge on to her sisters (Lowe 2003, 272–73).

In this context, the daughters and nieces of professional musicians had a distinct advantage: they could be taught expertly and for free at home by family members, with as secure a future ahead of them as any family could envisage. Should a marriage opportunity or court appointment not arise, they could find a home for life in a local convent, where they themselves could not only play and sing, but could also teach. This is presumably why we see generations of musician families associated with convents: Piccinini and Bassani nuns in Ferrara, Trombetti nuns in Bologna, Malvezzi nuns in Florence, and why Giaches de Wert's daughter becomes a celebrated organist.

3 Sound and Music in the Life of the Convent

Suor Clemenzia Sostegni's dispute with Archbishop Alessandro de' Medici over enclosure happened in the context of his ongoing programme of reform and restriction at Florence's convents. The *Trattato sopra il governo dei monasteri*, written in 1601 and addressed to his Vicar General in Florence, was designed to limit nuns' contact with the outside world as much as possible, and to deprive them of economic agency. The *Trattato*'s scope is wide, taking in every aspect of convent life from the quotidian (the arrangements for receiving and storing goods) and the economic (the fine details of how it is possible for a convent to manage finances when property is forbidden) to the extraordinary, such as demonic possession and punishments for extreme error (walling in the guilty nun). Its censorship rules tightly control nuns' exposure and response to cultural life outside the convent: how they communicated with their relatives, what books they could read, what music they could use in worship, and what they could do for recreation, including the way they incorporated music and drama into community celebrations.

A little over a hundred years previously, the revolutionary Dominican friar Girolamo Savonarola (d. 1498) castigated Florence's nuns (and its priests) for their use of organs and polyphony in the liturgy (Macey 1998). Savonarola nonetheless recognised the value of singing as a way of creating community and promoted instead the existing devotional practice of songs in vernacular Italian, called *laude*, which were accessible to both secular and religious worshippers.[41] The long tail of Savonarolan fervour amongst his followers reached well into the sixteenth century, and the *lauda* as a genre became particularly associated with nuns through the practices at Dominican convents such as the Paradiso in Florence and San Vincenzo in Prato (Macey 2007; Graca 2024). But polyphony flourished elsewhere in the city, and traces of its practice can be found in the records of many convents throughout the sixteenth and early seventeenth centuries (Gruppo di lavoro 'Firenze' 2006).

Apart from the Biffoli-Sostegni manuscript, there are no liturgical books or chronicles from San Matteo that provide direct evidence of its musical life, but sources such as the *Ricordanze*, Archbishop Alessandro's *Trattato*, the convent's late seventeenth-century *Sbozzo* of obligations, and its early eighteenth-century *Constituzioni* give enough secondary information to build a compelling picture.

3.1 Daily Sounds and Music

The 1713 *Constituzioni* creates both snapshots of the convent's present and a retrospective of its past, as both the rhythm and the sound of the life it describes were more or less unchanged from the time of the *Ricordanze*. San Matteo's relatively remote location meant that it was mostly undisturbed by the sounds that would have invaded more urban convents – which included 'words, conversations, desires, levity, and worldy profanity' that corrupted (8).[42] The rules around silence (to which an entire chapter is devoted) ensured that the convent's soundscape was predictable and fit for purpose, privileging the sound of the Divine Office above all others. The regularity of the bell was central to the daily routine within the convent's walls, calling the nuns to daily prayer – the

---

[41] The *lauda* is recorded from at least the end of the fourteenth century. It was flexible enough to be incorporated into processions, or public theatre, but respectable enough to form the basis of organised devotion, such as by the *laudesi* companies of fifteenth-century Florence (Leonardi 2021).

[42] In this section, page references in the primary source, the 1713 *Constituzioni*, will be given in parentheses. Silence was carefully regulated in early modern women's communities in Florence (Rombough 2024).

Constituzioni says that each nun should react to its sound as if she were hearing Christ's own voice (9). Outside, San Matteo's physical boundary would have been extended by the bell, its range welcoming a larger spiritual community. And if the bells fell silent, this damaged the convent's identity – among the punishments outlined in the *Trattato* for the unruliest convents was tying up their bells so that they could not be rung, externalising the convent's shame (343v).

The lives of choir nuns at any early modern convent were measured by music: the regular observance of the eight 'hours' of the Divine Office, plus the masses the nuns were obliged to hold, kept the community at prayer throughout day and night, every day of the year. Mostly, the hours were recited in chant, but on feast days the major hours (Vespers, Compline, Matins, and Lauds) and masses could contain polyphony and organ music. Somewhere between the practice of chant and polyphony was the practice of extemporised harmonisations of *canto fermo*, called *falsobordone*, which singers needed no notation to produce. Both festal and endowed masses could be – depending on the size of the endowment – solemn, sung, or said (*solenne*, *cantata*, *piane*). These terms related more to the involvement of male celebrants: in said masses, the priest did not chant, and the choir could say or sing their texts, or indeed sing something else entirely (Filippi 2017). Said and sung masses could be performed by the convent and their confessor alone, whereas solemn masses required additional priests to act as deacon and subdeacon.

The recitation of the Divine Office was, in essence, the nun's primary purpose on Earth: monastic institutions bore the responsibility for continuous prayer to safeguard their cities and communities in the protection of God, and to echo the choir of the angels for the faithful on Earth. The Divine Office did not require the presence of a priest. There were rules and advice regarding behaviour and performance, and how the Office sounded mattered, even in a rural convent like San Matteo. San Matteo's constitution required the nuns to:

> go with all speed and punctuality to Choir when the signal is heard, not making the others wait, or that they enter once the Office has begun, or that the number of singers is small, to the detriment of the divine praises, and the scandal of those who hear the scarcity of voices among so many nuns, and that they should sing distinctly, intelligibly without haste, without crashing the notes together ['senza frastuono di voci'], with the usual pauses, as befits the Divine Offices and to vocal prayers said in common; since they must know that reciting and singing in the Choir of the Holy Virgins is a an echo of the singing that the Angels make to God in Heaven; and since they sing in the presence of the same Angels as the Psalmist says, indeed in the presence of Jesus in the Blessed Sacrament, they must be careful not to give rise to confusion, to utter words, to burst into laughter, things that bring a certain

contempt for that Lord, before whom the present Angelic Spirits tremble with profound respect (28).[43]

The *Ricordanze* is silent on anything to do with daily worship, but it does contain references to obligations, both in terms of income and expenditure, but also in the scattered notes tucked in around the formal ledger. The *Constituzioni* situates obligations, whether sung or said, and especially prayers said for the deceased nuns, within the nuns' vow of charity (23). The 1694 *Sbozzo degli Obblighi* binds together both (some) originals and (more) clean copies of older documents. It is proof of the longevity of some endowments – in 1625, one Gianozzo Burci endowed an annual Mass for a minimum of 400 years, longer than the eventual life of the convent – and the sometimes difficult negotiations around when an obligation ceased. It also gives much more specific details of each obligation it records: Suor Orsina Cennini (d. 1579), for instance, used the income from a farm she inherited to endow two trentals (sets of thirty masses said on consecutive days), one to be said in the choir and the other in the infirmary, with white candles to be distributed to the singers, and a commemorative meal on the morning of the Purification of the Blessed Virgin Mary. While most obligations require at least one Office of the Dead and a single or combination of said, sung, and solemn Requiem Masses,[44] some testators ask for specific masses or set up quite complex instructions: Suor Laudomina Squarcialupi, who died in 1604, endowed three Masses for the Holy Trinity; in 1612 Domenico di Matteo Bindi, the Prior of the nearby church of San Michele a Monteripaldi, endowed a weekly Mass of the BVM during his life, and then after his death a weekly Requiem Mass, and a daily *De profundis* with the 'orazione sacerdotale' (the prayer *Fidelium*).

The *Ricordanze* also records payments to the friars who came to celebrate Mass: a single friar, most often the convent's confessor, for regular masses and multiple friars for solemn ones, such as those held on the feasts of San Lorenzo, Santa Chiara, and the Immaculate Conception. Sometimes these payments explicitly refer to singing. The annual *messa dei fratini* (see Section 2.1) required payment for six boys and their *maestro*; but also beginning in 1538, every year between *domenica dell'ulivo* (Palm Sunday) and *giovedì santo* (Maundy Thursday) there is a payment for the 'friars that come to sing the Passion', 'the Passionists' ('frati che venono cantorno e passi', 'i passionati'), or some other form of words, including 'the nuns and friars that sing the Passion' ('le monache et frati che cantorno el passio').

---

[43] Source Text 9.
[44] The scribe of the *Sbozzo* sometimes substituted 'messa cantata' for 'messa solenne' in the summary of the endowment she wrote at the bottom of each page, blurring the distinction between them.

The Mass Gospel on Palm Sunday, Holy Tuesday, and Holy Wednesday was an enactment of the Passions of Matthew, Mark, and Luke, with priest and deacon taking the role of the Evangelist narrator and Christ, and – in the simplest form – the subdeacon singing the words of all the other characters. However, a tradition of singing the words of the *turba* (the synagoga, or crowd) polyphonically existed in Florence from the fifteenth century, and Francesco Corteccia had composed a setting for the musicians of the cathedral, Santa Maria del Fiore, in 1527 (Sutherland 1972). There is no evidence either way to prove or disprove that the nuns of San Matteo sang the *turba*, but this form of collaboration was not unknown elsewhere in Europe (Volkhardt 2009).

3.2 The Practice of Music in Florence's Convents at the Turn of the Seventeenth Century

While clear records of women and men, specifically nuns and monks, singing polyphony together are rare, they do exist (Schwartz 2001). However, throughout the end of the sixteenth and the beginning of the seventeenth centuries, Florence's convents frequently employed male musicians to perform (in the public part of the church) when their own resources were lacking (Gruppo di lavoro 'Firenze' 2006). Alessandro de' Medici's *Trattato* explicitly forbade musical contact between men and women – not just men teaching at convents, but also nuns singing ('faccino Choro') with men 'as is normal in convents governed by friars', and – a particular abuse – nuns singing the Epistle when there was no deacon or subdeacon, as 'this is a grave error and must not be tolerated in any way' (339r).[45]

Archbishop Alessandro was not, in principle, opposed to nuns' music-making, but he was determined to control it (Lowe 2003, 273–78). On 24 March 1597, he wrote to his Vicar General, Antonio Benivieni,[46]

> I understand that in some of these convents a new form of music and singing has been introduced recently, with a single voice and the help of extraordinary musical instruments, with little edification of good people and against their institution. Therefore, my illustrious Lords and I have resolved to write to you how to deal with this. I and [the Bishop of] Arezzo have tried to provide that which is necessary by gradually removing the excess, so you will not fail to do, and God preserve you.

A month later, Benivieni issued a memorandum to all convents in the diocese:[47]

---

[45] Source Text 10. The prohibition on nuns singing the Epistle is common across Italy.
[46] I-Faav, Atti di monache 4, 24 March 1597; Source Text 11.
[47] I-Faav, Atti di monache 4, 24 April 1597; Source Text 12.

Reverend Mother Abbess

It seems that what is ordered in the service of God, and to motivate men to devotion, and to keep them in the Churches, sometimes turns into a worldly entertainment, and diverts from those good and devout purposes to which it was ordered to recite the Canonical hours. It also seems that in the distinction of these Canonical hours, the order of the Church is perverted by you to attract the support of the People, because Compline is celebrated with greater pomp than Vespers. Therefore, to repair similar faults and to prevent you from falling further into abuses, proceeding nevertheless with some discretion and distinction, you are commanded that from now on you use music with less melodic effort and ornaments, and more intelligible and closer to the chant. For now, therefore, you will be allowed to use all the keyboard instruments and a set of viols (with all four voices)[48] to help, supplement and bring out the consonance of your voices. Violins, lutes, and all wind instruments are prohibited, as well as singing with similar ornaments, vernacular materials, and individual voices, except settings of Latin Scripture with the organ. Thus, in addition to the edification of the good, many superfluous expenses will be avoided for individual nuns, and much waste of time and communication with men, by which they are distracted from the purpose of serving God, for which the same nuns have sequestered themselves from the world. And we will confirm the paternal and prudent warning and commandment that came to us from Rome on 24 March 1597, under penalty to you, in cases of transgression, of deprivation of office and rank, and be aware that it cannot be absolved except by us, our superior or successor. May God preserve you in his grace and keep you from error

From the Archbishop on 24 April 1597

[And under the greatest penalties we command you to publish and read in chapter this present letter of ours, so that no one can pretend ignorance.]

The archbishop's letter claimed that nuns were using a new style of composed music (*in canto figurato*), with a solo voice, or voices, accompanied by instruments that were not sanctioned by the Church. Alessandro was referring to monody (although this term is never used in the sixteenth and seventeenth centuries to describe new compositions for solo voice) and 'concertato' singing. Both the music and the method of performance had changed from that which the nuns had used previously, and Alessandro wanted to restore the status quo, however gradually. Benivieni's memorandum gives more detail in terms of what kinds of music were forbidden, what practices were deemed acceptable, and what the penalties would be if the convents did not comply. Highly ornamented solo singing was off the table, as were plucked strings, violins, and any wind instruments. Polyphony accompanied on the organ and viols was fine, so long as the words were intelligible, and ideally the chant melody was recognisable. Solo song was only permitted if it were in Latin and accompanied

---

[48] It is unclear here whether he means viols of all four sizes or doubling with viols on all four voices in a polyphonic texture.

only on the organ. The language of the memo is, in modern terms, passive-aggressive: we command you to do this, but at your discretion; but, if you fail to do this, we will deprive you of your office – and you are to read this out to everyone in chapter (a meeting of all the choir nuns) so that no one can pretend they do not know the rules.

Alessandro's orders regarding the use of the 'new form of music' predate the *Trattato* by four years. He did not include them in the later document, nor did he include them in the synodal decree of 1603, which outlines the basic rules for worship and sacraments for the whole archdiocese (Archdiocese of Florence 1603). But the *Trattato* mentions music and singing at several points, when discussing the architecture of the convent church; in setting out appropriate rules for chapel, and what music may be sung in which locations in the convent; and the in specific ceremony for delivering judgement on a community after a visitation.

The first quarter of the treatise deals with enclosure, the means for ensuring the nuns remained forever separate from the outside world. Although nuns were allowed to converse with outsiders in the *parlatorio*, these rooms were to be newly constructed with a door to the street and a wall of grates that could not be seen from the street, with no door leading into the convent (333v). In among the precise requirements for doors and screens, which would prevent even a slip of paper being passed through, are disparaging comments about the vogue for high choir galleries in the convent's churches where the nuns could be both out of sight and yet easily heard – instead of an inner choir, separated from the outer church by a wall with grated windows. There is also an instruction for organs to be placed so that they are behind iron bars with the keyboard behind the pipes, in a space with a lockable door, so that not just any nun could access it for practice. It continues, 'it would be better if they [the organs] were all inside the choir, and that the sound went out through the grates, from where the voices and the psalmody come out, but since it is very expensive, I could not order them to be moved' (335r).[49]

Alessandro felt that the greatest risk of interaction might occur during the observance of the offices and of masses, whether that interaction was with the public or with priests. In addition to the ban on male/female musical interactions in the convent, he asks his vicar to ensure that convents observe the hours at the appropriate time, especially Matins, which should not be sung either at dawn or just at nightfall – presumably so that outsiders would not congregate to hear the singing, as they would for Vespers and (to Alessandro's consternation) Compline (338v–339r). So that they do not need to invite more priests than

---

[49] Source Text 13.

necessary to celebrate Solemn Mass, he gives convents where there is no tradition of music permission only to chant, rather than hiring additional singers or encouraging them to introduce new musical practice. He also sees feast days as a temptation to other kinds of excess: 'I would remind you that on feast days, no great expenditure should be made on the vestments, no money should be spent on music, no priests should be given food (but instead outsiders should be paid), and the same thing should be observed in the vestition of the nuns and similar occasions' (338r).[50]

Married women and widows were forbidden to enter the convent, except with the pope's permission. Unmarried women were allowed to enter the convent as boarders, but if they left for any reason, they would not normally be allowed to re-enter the same convent. The *Trattato* restates a ban, made by memorandum in 1583,[51] that no licenses for boarders or novices would be granted between Christmas and Lent, because girls were entering the convents just for the entertainments and leaving before Lent (336v).[52] But Alessandro did not wish to ban entertainments altogether, as he saw them as a necessary comfort for women who have severed all contact with the world. He sanctioned a variety of different kinds of representations, including processions, tableaux, year-round Nativity scenes, and plays on Bible stories or the lives of the saints. Scripts were to be vetted, and nuns were not allowed to skip the Office to perform, nor were they allowed to remove their habit, wear men's clothes, or grow their hair out to represent a secular woman (337v–338r).[53]

Convent theatre had been an important element of Florentine culture for centuries, providing an opportunity for nuns to practice a range of creative talents: poetry, music, acting, visual arts, dance, even costumery. Its most ancient roots lay in the drama of the Christmas and Easter stories, but by the turn of the seventeenth century many convents engaged in fully realised dramatic productions, with multi-act plays written by both outsiders and the nuns themselves.[54] The word 'rappresentatione' could encompass a variety of forms, however: Suor Annalena Aldobrandini's *veglie* from the convent of San Giorgio di Spirito Santo alla Costa include spoken poetic 'disputes', musical floats in procession, audience participation games, and breaks for refreshments (Stras 2012). These entertainments were part of the social calendar, often coinciding with the city's traditional festivals, such as Carnival and Calendimaggio: secular

---

[50] Source Text 14.   [51] I-Faav, Professioni di monache 2 (1582–1585), s.f.
[52] Source Text 15.   [53] Source Text 16.
[54] Elissa Weaver comprehensively surveyed this cultural practice (Weaver 2002). Tim Carter has recently argued that two of Ottavio Rinuccini's librettos, *Dafne* (music by Jacopo Corsi, Jacopo Peri, and perhaps Giulio Caccini) and *Arianna* (with music by Claudio Monteverdi) may have been produced in Florentine convents in the 1610s (Carter 2024, para. 3.8–3.14).

visitors, especially women, would enter the cloister to join the audience of older nuns – younger nuns and novices mostly made up the performing troupes.

One hundred years later, the *Constituzioni* also sets out requirements for Carnival entertainments: that they are approved by the abbess and the confessor, that they do not require nuns to change their clothes or appearance, and that they do not disturb private devotions or public services, unlike the secular plays, games, dances, and parties that last long into the night. Should such diversions still sound too tempting, the author recalls that the Lord told S. Maria Maddalena de' Pazzi (a famous sixteenth-century Florentine nun) that nuns who participated in that kind of indecency would be eternally damned (20).

Many sources associated with convents show that, despite repeated attempts to limit nuns' interactions with the outside world, secular culture freely permeated the convents' enclosure: this is particularly well demonstrated by the retexting of secular songs, both popular tunes and composed madrigals, into *laude*, songs with spiritual texts in the vernacular Italian. Communal devotional singing had been embedded in Florentine social and religious practice since the thirteenth century through the activities of the *laudesi* companies, and took on particular significance during the Savonarolan republic (Wilson 1992; Macey 1998; Wilson 2009). Many of the *laude* published by Serafino Razzi in 1563 and dedicated to Suor (later Saint) Caterina Ricci, the abbess of San Vincenzo in Prato, took their melodies from fifteenth-century Carnival songs, but the aristocratic nuns of San Vincenzo also had access to Florence's unpublished madrigal repertoire through their families (Macey 2007). *Laude* could be used in various contexts in the convent: for an audience as part of an entertainment, such as those by Suor Annalena; as part of an organised devotional event, such as a procession or a gathering in front of an altar or statue; and as an accompaniment to manual labour. The *Trattato* allowed these last two uses, provided they took place in the inner convent, away from the ears of the public (338v).[55]

3.3 Music and Sound in Devotions and Rites

The *Ricordanze* makes only passing mention of two ceremonies that would have certainly contained music: 'velazione' or vestition, and 'sacrazione', or profession of a novice, in which she made her final vows and became a full member of the community. These could be very elaborate affairs, and at more prestigious convents within the city walls, external musicians were often hired by the family to ensure a young woman a more opulent transition from one state to the next (see Section 4.5).

---

[55] Source Text 17.

The *Constituzioni* mentions processions in general, which happened on Sundays and 'on other occasions throughout the year'. But it is more specific about the nature of its communal devotional gatherings, or 'visits' (*visite*). These happened weekly on Fridays in front of the Crucifix,[56] and on Saturdays before the Virgin Mary; and before the Oratorio of the Infant Jesus (perhaps a painting or a Nativity set – the adoration of the Nativity was a particular Franciscan practice) on the twenty-fifth of every month. The visits were held by the whole community, and involved the singing of 'litanies, psalms, hymns, laude, and prayers' appropriate for each occasion (31–32).[57] The regularity of these visits, and the requirement for the full participation of the convent community, suggests that the texts spoken and music sung would have been committed to memory, perhaps even passed down from generation to generation.

The capacity for collective recitation and singing to promote order, discipline, conformity, and what the constitution calls 'the beautiful harmony of all the religious virtues' (13) seems part of what made a community run like clockwork: 'the individuals and matters of a community are like the many wheels of a clock, and the disorder of one puts all in disorder' (27).[58] These qualities would certainly have been useful in the context of the ceremony accompanying the end of a visitation, the last mention of music in the *Trattato*. At the beginning, the nuns went into the chapterhouse carrying lit candles, intoning the hymn *Veni Creator Spiritus*. The archbishop's vicar delivered his initial observations and recommendations to the abbess and the community, who then sang the *Te Deum*, the ubiquitous hymn of thanksgiving, at the end of his address.

The *Constituzioni* outlines two additional ceremonies, and it is difficult to know when they first became part of San Matteo's year (32–33). On New Year's Eve, the choir nuns came together and recited the *Miserere* (Psalm 50/51) and disciplined themselves (that is, self-mortification) while praying for forgiveness for their and the world's ingratitude; once finished, they intoned the *Te Deum*. Then, after three more days of further meditation and mortification, on the morning of Epiphany (6 January), all the professed nuns, both choir and servant, met in the choir to say the *Confiteor* (the prayer of confession) and to receive absolution. They then collectively renewed their vows, speaking loudly in unison. The formula for the renewal is printed with asterisks denoting pauses, which the nuns are obliged to observe ('fermandosi alle pause'), ensuring a collective and orderly enunciation.

---

[56] San Matteo's crucifix is now in the parish church of Santa Margherita a Montici. It was venerated for performing miracles, and was paraded 'in times of need' (Santoni 1847, 119).
[57] Source Text 18.   [58] Source Text 19.

Prostrated at your feet,* oh my divine Spouse,* I beg your forgiveness for the omissions* committed by me in the past year,* in the exact observance of my vows.* And longing with their renewal* to renew my spirit in the new year,* in the presence of all the Heavenly Court* and especially of Mary, eternal Virgin* most lovely Lady* Advocate,* and my Mother,* of the Virgins' Apostle Saint Matthew,* of the Father Saint Francis,* of the Mother Saint Clare,* and of my Holy Guardian Angel,* I make a perpetual vow of Poverty, * of Chastity,* of Obedience.* Meanwhile, I beg you, oh my sweet Jesus,* to accept this my offering,* as you accepted from the Magi* the symbols of these three Vows,* that is Gold,* Myrrh,* and Incense,* and to grant me* a true change of life,* symbolised by the change of Path,* that the Magi made after their gift,* so that travelling by the new path of perfection* I may arrive in Heaven* that you have made my Country, and Homeland.* Amen (34).[59]

4 The Music of the Biffoli-Sostegni Manuscript

Early modern music manuscripts often represent much more than the musical information they contain. While the repertoire is the primary or most immediate focus of the reader, many more issues or questions lie just behind the music: how the music was collected, the order in which it appears, the precision of the copying, the meaning of any non-musical information or images, and so on. The Biffoli-Sostegni manuscript has an index prepared by the copyist; some works appear to be grouped together; there are few obvious copying errors; and its presentation – with a decorative scheme that includes images of nuns and references to their names and relationships – suggests that the copyist was mindful of the community in which his work would reside.

But the music, too, is entwined with the convent's history and identity. While much of it would be useful to any religious establishment, male or female, some is specific to worship in a convent of Poor Clares, and some of it could have been written for, or even by, the nuns of San Matteo. Moreover, it is possible to find correspondences between some of the works and events described by the historical sources relating to San Matteo, giving us a richer – if still conjectural – understanding of how music figured in the lives of its nuns.

4.1 Equal-Voice Music

Although the Biffoli-Sostegni repertoire shows great variety in genre and style, it is unified by its consistent use of a limited vocal range, known as *voci pari* (equal-voice) composition. *Voci pari* polyphony is music written for more than one voice

---

[59] Source Text 20.

that can be sung by a single-sex group of adult singers, such as might be found in a chapel that employed no boy singers, or in a female convent. *Voci pari* could be notated in low (Bass and Tenor) or high (Alto and Treble) clefs, but since competent singers could read any clef, repertoire composed in one single-sex environment could readily be adopted in another. Nonetheless, the copyist's choice of clef can hint at a work's origin or the composer's inspiration: of the manuscript's seventy-eight works, around a third (twenty-three) are written in low clefs, perhaps because they originated in an all-male environment, or because they incorporate a liturgical chant – which are almost invariably notated in low clefs – as one of the voices. The rest are in high clefs, suggesting that they were composed expressly for high voices.[60]

Voci pari polyphony was set apart from other styles even during the sixteenth century. Theorists and teachers writing composition treatises tended to avoid using *voci pari* works as illustrations and relegated the discussion of *voci pari* technique to supplementary paragraphs or chapters, because although *voci pari* composition is subject to the same rules as *voci piene* (literally, full voices) it is much more likely to bend those rules because of the proximity of the parts. Moreover, publishers began to issue *voci pari* works in separate volumes, potentially to create and preserve a new market for the format (Stras 2017b, 617–19). Nuns could arrange *voci piene* works by playing the bass part on an instrument (in Italy, usually the organ or a bass viol, or both), by transposing all or some of the voices, or combining these approaches. However, for a small convent such as San Matteo, a repertoire of *voci pari* music would be ideal, as it would rely less on there being a bass instrument in the convent or a nun to play it.[61]

The range of any individual work in the Biffoli-Sostegni manuscript is never more than a sixteenth (two octaves plus one note) and is usually less than two octaves. The repertoire exhibits the broad sonic characteristics of *voci pari* music: transitory and unresolved dissonances; the sound (if not the reality) of voices moving in block chords created by voices in the same register crossing each other; and a sense of harmonic stasis created by the same phrase being repeated in close imitation by four voices in turn (Stras 2017b, 642–57). Most of the manuscript's four-voice works, regardless of their length, exploit at least two, if not all three of these techniques.

---

[60] *Voci pari* high clefs were used much less frequently than low clefs, particularly for sacred works: some high-clef music transmitted in earlier sources was even transposed into low clefs in later publications, but the reverse does not happen (Johnstone 2006, 35–40).

[61] The audio examples in this Element use a variety of strategies: voices alone; voices doubled on organ; voices with some parts played on viol, lute, or both; all voices doubled on organ with the Bassus doubled on viol.

4.2 The Masses

The most substantial works in manuscript are the two Mass Ordinary settings, one in four voices and the other in three.[62] They are both what have been called 'parody masses', works based on a pre-existing musical model that could be either secular or sacred.[63] While modern musicians and listeners have to work to understand the implications and resonances of this kind of composition, in its original context the musicians and listeners could experience a mass as a real-time musical event at the same time as summoning the memory of the model (Milsom 2020, 252). This blending of meaning had the potential to imbue liturgical worship with specific affect – and in the case of the two Biffoli-Sostegni masses, with elements of the convent's recent history that manifested its reliance on divine intervention.

The four-voice *Messa sopra Recordare Virgo Mater* is the first work in the manuscript (1v–14r); it is followed by the motet from which it is modelled. The anonymous *Recordare Virgo Mater* sets the Mass Offertory for the Feast of the Immaculate Conception and its prosa, *Ab hac familia*. The prosa petitions the Virgin to intercede to God on behalf of a community, using the metaphor of life as the sinner's journey homewards towards Heaven. The *Messa con tre voci* (hereafter *Messa sopra Je le lerray*) begins the manuscript's three-voice section, but its model is not included or identified. This is unsurprising, since the model is a secular French chanson that tells of domestic violence and imprisonment, and (probably) adultery. *Je le lerray puisqu'il me bat* circulated in manuscripts dating from the first decades of the sixteenth century, in one-, three-, and four-voice versions. A three-voice version attributed to the French court composer Antoine de Févin is included in a Florentine collection that was probably compiled in the late 1510s or early 1520s (I-Fn Magliabechiano XIX.117, 6v–7r).[64]

Both mass models seem to speak to the condition of the convent during the Siege of Florence between October 1529 and August 1530, when the nuns had been evacuated from their estate to the plague-ridden city and billeted in the house of an exiled Florentine noble. *Recordare Virgo Mater* pleads for an entire household, referring also to a state of exile or being far from home; *Je le lerray*

---

[62] The Mass Ordinary is the five sections of the liturgy that are consistent in every service: Kyrie, Gloria, Credo, Sanctus, and Agnus Dei.

[63] Musicologist John Milsom calls these 'T-Masses', created with 'intentional acts of *transferring* and *transforming* text-bearing polyphonic ideas, and usually also with the *transfusion* of concepts from model to Mass' (Milsom 2018, 320).

[64] Thanks to Bonnie Blackburn for her help in identifying the model chanson. A monophonic version exists in the Bayeux manuscript, F-Pn 9346, 67v. A transcription of Févin's arrangement, as well as a full text and translation are available on Peter Woetmann Christoffersen's *The Uppsala Chansonnier MS76a*, http://uppsala.pwch.dk/Upp043.html, accessed 9 May 2025.

recounts the experience of aggression, captivity, and potentially even espionage in a feminine voice. The *Messa sopra Recordare* may well have had an additional importance for San Matteo through its relationship to a motet for the Immaculate Conception. When Dianora de' Parigi endowed her obligation in thanks for God's protection from harm after lightning struck the convent bell-gable, she specified a Mass of the Immaculate Conception (see Section 2.1). While there is no proof that the *Messa sopra Recordare* was the music used for the service, its placement at the beginning of the manuscript, before even the music for St Matthew or St Clare, suggests it was hugely significant to the nuns.

These two works are unusual in the sixteenth-century repertoire, for different reasons: the *Messa sopra Recordare* because it is almost unique as mass setting for four equal voices notated in high clefs (there are low equal-voice masses in circulation, but not many); the *Messa sopra Je le lerray* because it is a three-voice mass based on a chanson that uses the compositional technique of imitative counterpoint. While there are plenty of three-voice masses from the later fifteenth century based on chansons, no other treats the model as the basis for pervasive imitative polyphony, as found in the four-voice mass from the late fifteenth century onwards.

The *Messa sopra Recordare* serves as an excellent introduction to the sound-world of early sixteenth-century *voci pari* polyphony. The motet's opening *soggetto*, or subject, is introduced in imitation at the unison in all four parts: starting with the Bassus, then Tenor, then Altus, and finally Cantus (Example 1a/Audio 1a). In the mass, this opening is cited exactly only in the Sanctus, but the voices are reordered: Bassus, Altus, Cantus, Tenor (Example 1b/Audio 1b). By stacking the melody onto itself, the imitation creates static block sonorities that sound like forbidden parallels – even though any two voices never actually move in parallel fifths, because the voices are all in the same range, the fifths are heard

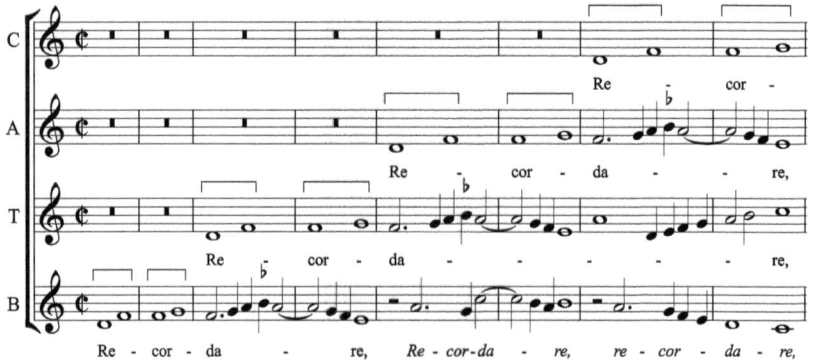

Example/Audio 1a B-Bc 27766: 14v–15r, *Recordare Virgo Mater*, bb. 1–8. Audio file available at www.cambridge.org/stras

Example/Audio 1b B-Bc 27766: 8v–9r, *Messa sopra Recordare Virgo Mater*, Sanctus, bb. 1–8. Audio file available at www.cambridge.org/stras

Example/Audio 1c Sounding chords of *Messa sopra Recordare Virgo Mater*, Sanctus, bb. 1–8. Audio file available at www.cambridge.org/stras

(Example 1c/Audio 1c). This happens first at the end of b. 5, when the Bassus rises to a *c*, the music's first aural surprise. It barely avoids parallel fifths with the voice entering beneath it; moreover, the *c* hints at a dissonant seventh because the *d* root is already firmly established in the listener's ear.

The other four sections of the *Messa sopra Recordare* – the Kyrie, Gloria, Credo, and Agnus Dei – paraphrase the model's opening in ways that exploit that aural surprise, perhaps acknowledging that this moment would be the one that stayed in the listener's memory (aptly, occurring on the word *recordare* 'remember'). The implied seventh becomes real in b. 7 of the Kyrie and the Credo (Example 2a and Example 2c/Audio 2a and Audio 2c); these two openings are essentially the same apart from some adjustments in rhythm to accommodate the text. The Gloria emphasises the stepwise sounding parallels by repeating them in bb. 5–6 and bb 7–8 (Example 2b/Audio 2b). The Agnus finally leans into the dissonance by delaying but then intensifying it (Example 3/Audio 3). In b. 8 the Altus and Cantus form the *d*–*c* interval, following it immediately, if fleetingly, with another seventh *c*–*b*, before resting at the end of the bar on a second (the inversion of a seventh) *g*–*a* between Tenor and Altus.

The model's opening, however memorable and striking, is used only at the beginning of each mass section. The rest of the mass uses melodic fragments from the model in different ways but also sets up its own terms of reference for stimulating the listener's memory: see, for instance, the octave leaps in b. 7 of

Example/Audio 2a B-Bc 27766: 1v–2r, *Messa sopra Recordare Virgo Mater*, Kyrie, bb. 1–8. Audio file available at www.cambridge.org/stras

Example/Audio 2b B-Bc 27766: 2v–3r, *Messa sopra Recordare Virgo Mater*, Gloria, bb. 1–8. Audio file available at www.cambridge.org/stras

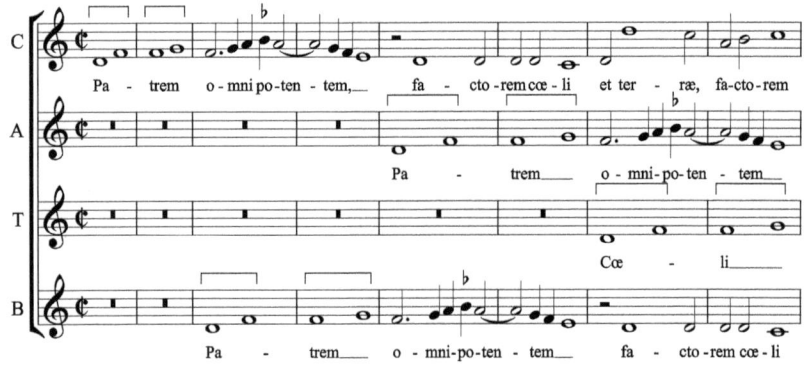

Example/Audio 2c B-Bc 27766: 5v–6r, *Messa sopra Recordare Virgo Mater*, Credo, bb. 1–8. Audio file available at www.cambridge.org/stras

Example/Audio 3 B-Bc 27766: 8v–9r, *Messa sopra Recordare Virgo Mater*, Agnus, bb. 1–9. Audio file available at www.cambridge.org/stras

the Kyrie (Example 2a/Audio 2a) and b. 5 of the Gloria (Example 2b/Audio 2b), which never appear in the model.

The *Messa sopra Je le lerray*, in contrast, resembles most closely a style of composition Cynthia Cyrus calls 'chanson reworkings', which she identifies as a secular, largely Florentine phenomenon of the late fifteenth and early sixteenth centuries (Cyrus 1990, 4–5). It uses the melody of its chanson model consistently and in its entirety, along with the contrapuntal material of Févin's three-voice arrangement. The close relationship between chanson and mass then creates a different frame for memory – one that does not just rely on affect and intent ('recordare') but potentially on the experience of hearing/singing the original chanson and the context in which that happened.

The melody of *Je le lerray* is in three sections, the first two comprising two lines each, and the third reprising the first line as a refrain (Example 4a/Audio 4a).[65] Févin's arrangement adds two accompanying voices to the melody, and repeats the final refrain, creating the musical form ABA1 (Example 4b/Audio 4b). The Kyrie of the mass retains this three-part structure, embedding the first two lines of the melody in the first 'Kyrie eleison' (Example 5a/Audio 5a); the second two lines in the 'Christe eleison' (Example 5b/Audio 5b); and the refrain in the second 'Kyrie eleison'. From the start, then, the whole of the chanson is evoked as God's mercy is invoked. The Kyrie also incorporates the identifying characteristics of *voci pari* polyphony: harmonic stasis (bb. 22–27), multiple dissonances (b. 31), and parallels (Example 6/Audio 6, b. 75) – although here they are actual, and not virtual, parallel fifths.

---

[65] Please note, audio examples are not always sung at the pitch indicated by the music examples, which are transcribed at the pitch given in the manuscript. Transposition to suit available vocal forces is a well-documented aspect of early modern performance practice; see (Stras 2017a; 2024).

Example/Audio 4a F-Pn 9346, 67v: *Je le lerray puisqu'il me bat*.
Audio file available at www.cambridge.org/stras

Example/Audio 4b I-Fn Magl XIX.117, 6v–7r: Antoine de Févin, *Je le lerray puisqu'il me bat*, bb. 1–11. Audio file available at www.cambridge.org/stras

If a comprehensive memory of the three-voice chanson and its association (Florence's besiegement) is summoned by its use in the mass, the memory could have been supplemented by the composer's choice of a new melody, unrelated to the chanson, for the 'Qui tollis peccata mundi' section of the Gloria. Although the melody starts like the chanson's B section, its continuation takes it up instead of down (Example 7a/Audio 7a). This melody, transposed up a tone, is identical to the opening subject of Phillipe Verdelot's motet 'Recordare, Domine', a work transmitted in two manuscript sources – one of which was copied by Antonio Moro – that contain repertoire intimately entangled in the politics of 1520s Florence (Example 7b/Audio 7b). Verdelot's motet calls for

Example/Audio 5a B-Bc 27766, 135v–136r: *Messa sopra Je le lerray*, Kyrie, bb. 1–11. Audio file available at www.cambridge.org/stras

Example/Audio 5b B-Bc 27766, 136v–137r: *Messa sopra Je le lerray*, Kyrie, bb. 23–32. Audio file available at www.cambridge.org/stras

God's help to 'an end to external war, famine, and pestilence' and may have been composed between 1527 and 1530, when Florence was ravaged by plague and conflict (Ryan 2019, 308). Its inclusion would potentially have reinforced

Example/Audio 6 B-Bc 27766, 137v–138r: *Messa sopra Je le lerray*, Kyrie, bb. 74–79. Audio file available at www.cambridge.org/stras

Example/Audio 7a B-Bc 27766, 137v–138r: *Messa sopra Je le lerray*, Gloria, bb. 47–59. Audio file available at www.cambridge.org/stras

the contextual meaning of the mass for Florentine citizens who had lived through the siege – again, the word *recordare* brings a powerful resonance.

While these two masses arise from very different models, there is one a spectacular similarity between them: in the Sanctus of both works, a canon at the unison using the same melodic fragment features in two subsections, the Pleni (at 'gloria tua') and the Osanna. It appears only once in a single voice in each model and barely features elsewhere in either mass. It is not an unusual melody; it is, however, curious that it crops up in only these places, and in exactly the same places, in two works that are otherwise so utterly different. At

Example/Audio 7b I-Rv 35–40, n. 26: Phillipe Verdelot, *Recordare Domine*, bb. 1–6. Audio file available at www.cambridge.org/stras

a stretch, this similarity could suggest that the composer of one mass knew the other mass, or even that the masses are by the same composer. But it is perhaps less contentious to suggest that the nuns, who would have known and sung these mass settings, themselves would have formed the connection; far from obvious on the page, the echoes are much clearer after repeated listening.

4.3 Other Music for the Mass

Because the Ordinary comprises those sections of the Mass that are common to every day's worship, it the most recognisable element and the one that receives the most attention from composers. However, there are other portions of the liturgy – the propers, or those that are specific to a feast or a time of year – that can be set to music. There are only a handful of proper settings in the Biffoli-Sostegni manuscript, all of which pertain to important feasts in the convent's calendar. *Hæc dies quam fecit* is the Gradual for Easter Sunday; *Recordare Virgo Mater* is the Offertory for the Feast of the Immaculate Conception; *Portas cœli aperuit* is the Offertory for the fourth day of the Octave of Easter (although its second part, *Hic est panis*, is not).[66] There are two Gospels: *In illo tempore: Thomas unus de duodecim* (for the Octave of Easter, also the Feast of St Thomas, Apostle) and *In illo tempore: dixit Jesus* (for the Feast of St Matthew). These works may not have been sung as part of the Mass liturgy, but we cannot rule out that they – or indeed any of the antiphons or hymns

---

[66] *Hic est panis* is the second half of a responsory (*Ego sum panis vitae*) for Corpus Christi, hinting that this two-part motet had a paraliturgical purpose.

included in the manuscript – were sung during a Mass. Non-liturgical motets had long had a place during Mass worship, specifically at the Offertory, the Elevation, and at Communion (Cummings 1981, 45). But even the Low, or Said, Mass – a prime constituent of the many masses the nuns were obliged to hold on behalf of donors, as well as part of their daily worship – could be accompanied by any suitable music (Filippi 2017).

4.4 Music for the Divine Office

The Divine Office, or Opus Dei, was the principal spiritual occupation for monastic institutions, a framework of regular, collective prayer that ensured all the psalms of the Old Testament were recited throughout the week. Unlike the Mass, which could be spoken, the Divine Office was always sung. It was divided into eight services, or hours, spread across the day to allow for other activities, such as other forms of worship, labour, learning, sleeping, and eating.

Nearly all the Office music in the Biffoli-Sostegni manuscript belongs to the service of Vespers. The sixteenth-century monastic Vespers combined fixed elements, the most significant of which was the Magnificat (the Canticle of the BVM), with other elements that changed according to the day. Like the Mass, Office liturgies had antiphons and hymns that were appropriate to specific feast days, and more regular sets of psalms that would be used for specific categories of feasts – for instance, if it were the feast day of a virgin saint, or an apostle. Psalms were invariably paired with an antiphon that was sung both before and after the doxology ('Gloria Patri et Filio et Spiritui Sancto. Sicut erat in principio et nunc et semper, et in sæcula sæculorum. Amen') that concluded every psalm and canticle.

The music of the Divine Office was similarly a mix of the regular and the specific. While many antiphons and hymns had distinctive chants, some melodies were adapted to a range of different texts. In their simplest form, the psalms and the Magnificat were recited to one of eight different sequences of notes called psalmtones, distinguished from each other by the specific combination of their beginnings (intonations, or *exordia*), the note on which the bulk of the verse was recited (the dominant or *tenor*), and their endings (terminations, or *differentiæ*). Fluent psalmody relied on memorisation, not just of the tone but also of the psalms themselves; hence often an entire chanted service could be notated with just the antiphons and abbreviated instructions for the psalms, with an indication of their tones and *differentiae*.

Alongside the festal Mass, Vespers offered convents and public worshippers the best opportunity for making and hearing music. Polyphonic settings of the Magnificat, and of the psalms for major feast days, are common in the sixteenth-century repertoire. Mostly, these settings are *alternatim*; that is, only alternate verses are set to polyphony, leaving the remaining verses to be sung as chant alone – these chant verses are not notated, but would have been sung from memory. Magnificat antiphons, too, are frequently set polyphonically: as the highlight of the service, they could also function outside the liturgy as a musical symbol of the saint or the feast. The Magnificat itself was the daily repetition, surely significant to nuns, of the BVM's declaration of her life's commitment to God.

Vespers is the first service of the festal cycle, sung in the late afternoon the day before the official feast day. As it signalled the end of the working day for many of the faithful, it also anticipated the following morning's celebration: for the most solemn feasts, after the physical and spiritual challenges of the night offices of Matins and Lauds, the nuns could look forward to a more generous breakfast.

4.4.1 The Psalms and Magnificats

In the four-voice section of the manuscript, there are three sets of Vespers psalms and three settings of the Magnificat; a three-voice Magnificat by Jehan de Billon, one of the few works in the manuscript that has a concordance and attribution in a contemporary print, appears on its own at the end of the three-voice section (it is unattributed in the manuscript). The eighteen four-voice works represent a compendium of compositional styles popular in Florence in the mid sixteenth century. They range from the most austere harmonisations of the psalmtone – so basic they could have been extemporised without music – through unprepossessing, mostly homophonic settings that state the text clearly and succinctly, to grander and more intricate imitative polyphony that moves away from the tone to create a more impressive musical event.

The four-voice psalms and Magnificats are organised into three sets that suggest how they may have been used at the convent, for they present items for specific feast days in the correct order for the liturgy. The first set, for Vespers 1 of the Common of Saints, is followed in the manuscript by the hymn for the Feast of St Matthew, then a Magnificat; the second set, for the Common of Virgins and the BVM, is followed by the Vespers 2 hymn for St Clare, a Magnificat, and then the Vespers 2 Magnificat antiphon for Clare. The third set, for Vespers 2 of the Common of Saints has no hymn but it, too, is immediately followed by a Magnificat. The copyist may have initiated this sequencing, but equally, the music may have been given to him in the convent's own discrete gatherings.

Approaching these often short, functional works as miniatures of performance, not just composition, shows even a convent with limited resources –

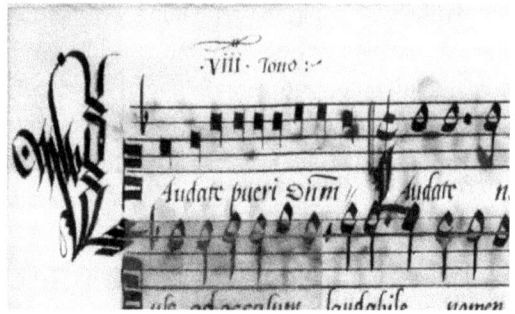

Figure 7 B-Bc 27766, 48v: *Laudate pueri*, Cantus, indication of psalm tone and transposition (Bibliothèque du Conservatoire royal de Bruxelles).

a choir, an organ, and an optional bass instrument – could create reasonable musical variety for worshippers. In most of them, at least one polyphonic verse is written for reduced – three, or even two – voices. But the choirmistress would have had other choices she could make: solo voices can be used instead of a full choir; a bass instrument can often replace or support the lowest voice. Moreover, the works' presentation in the manuscript can reveal more about the way music was created for and performed by convent choirs.

The set for the Common of Virgins offers some opportunities for illustration. The second psalm, the *Laudate pueri*, has an indication that it is in the Eighth Tone (*VIII tono*), in this case transposed up a seventh (Figure 7).[67] This would tell the nuns how to intone the alternate verses, since the Second and Eighth Tones effectively share the same intonation, although notated starting on different pitches. The intonations are not always given by the copyist, and when they are, they are mostly notated without any regard for word stresses; however, in some, he indicates a rhythm by using different note shapes. For the fourth psalm *Nisi Dominus*, also on the Eighth Tone, the note shapes appear to indicate faster intonation of the word 'ædificaverit' and a longer first syllable of the word 'domum' (Figure 8).

The *Laudate pueri*, like most in the set, is predominantly homophonic, with all voices delivering the text simultaneously in a chordal texture. The upper two voices often cross each other and stay close to the psalmtone; the lower two voices offer harmonic support, the Bassus always providing the root (Example 8/Audio 8). The *Nisi Dominus* is more polyphonically conceived than the other four psalms, with the top three voices in identical ranges sharing responsibility for maintaining the recitation tenor (Example 9/Audio 9). In all

---

[67] The reason for this transposition is a mystery: It may have aided the transition from psalm to antiphon, but it is certainly not to accommodate the ranges of the choir, since the *Nisi Dominus* and the Magnificat of the set are also on the Eighth Tone, but untransposed.

Figure 8 B-Bc 27766, 50v: *Nisi Dominus*, Cantus, apparent rhythm in intonation (Bibliothèque du Conservatoire royal de Bruxelles).

Example/Audio 8 B-Bc 27766, 48v–49r: *Laudate pueri*, bb. 6–15.
Audio file available at www.cambridge.org/stras

but the first verse, the voices enter in imitation, and in the doxology the composer uses close imitation at the unison, creating the harmonic stasis signature of equal-voice polyphony (Example 10/Audio 10, bb. 51–54). The setting also shows a degree of attention to the meaning of the words at 'Vanum est vobis' (Example 9/Audio 9). The note B flat (*b molle*, or soft B), when it alters a B natural that has already been sung, is often used expressively (Blackburn 2015). Here, it lends not only an acknowledgement of vanity and performative asceticism, but also a subtle knowingness in terms of the verse's meaning for religious life: the King James Version reads, 'It is vain for you to rise up early, to sit up late, to eat the bread of sorrows: for so he giveth his beloved sleep'.

Example/Audio 9 B-Bc 27766, 50v–51r: *Nisi Dominus*, bb. 9–26.
Audio file available at www.cambridge.org/stras

The Magnificat bundled with the Common of Virgins is also on the Eighth Tone and is composed in imitative polyphony throughout. Because the tone has limited material from which to create the imitative subjects (effectively just the intonation and the termination), the Magnificat appears to share material with the *Nisi Dominus*: compare the opening of the 'Sicut erat' of the Magnificat with the 'Gloria Patri' of the psalm (Example 11/Audio 11; Example 10/Audio 10, bb. 42–47). But the Magnificat also uses the compositional technique of *cantus firmus*, in which one voice intones the verse in long notes while the others engage in imitative polyphony: in the 'Quia fecit mihi magna' the Cantus has the psalmtone (Example 12/Audio 12). *Cantus firmus* composition was, by the middle of the sixteenth century, a somewhat old-fashioned technique, yet still part of a composer's education: this Magnificat's careful display of a range of

Example/Audio 10 B-Bc 27766, 50v–51r: *Nisi Dominus*, bb. 42–54.
Audio file available at www.cambridge.org/stras

Example/Audio 11 B-Bc 27766, 58v–59r: *Magnificat ottavo tono*, bb. 193–98.
Audio file available at www.cambridge.org/stras

Example/Audio 12 B-Bc 27766, 58v–59r: *Magnificat ottavo tono*, bb. 43–75.
Audio file available at www.cambridge.org/stras

skills might suggest it was composed by someone still learning their craft, potentially even a nun at San Matteo.

Another psalm on the Eighth Tone, the third psalm of Vespers 2 for the Common of Saints, *In convertendo*, presents yet another way in which psalms could be sung in choir – in unmeasured block chords that nonetheless indicate

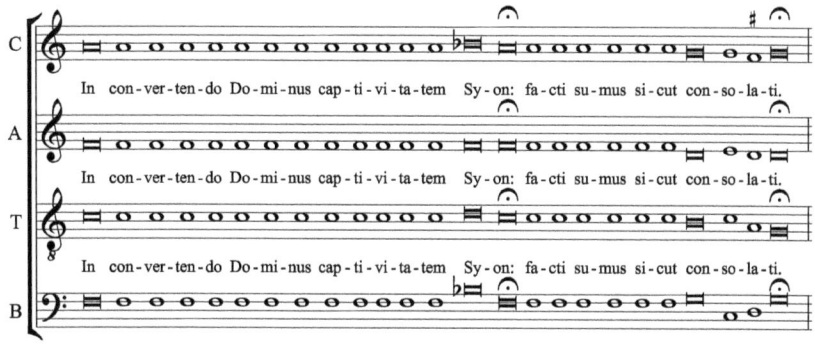

Example/Audio 13 B-Bc 27766, 113v–113(bis)r: *In convertendo*, b. 1.
Audio file available at www.cambridge.org/stras

stresses on longer notes (Example 13/Audio 13). This setting has the psalmtone (without the intonation) in the Tenor voice; the other parts are created by common rules for extemporising harmonies known variously as *falsobordone* or *contrappunto alla mente*. These rules advise on the intervals the individual voices should make from the Tenor: for instance, the Bassus can alternate fifths and thirds, but can also use octaves and unisons. These rules would allow even moderately skilled ensembles to create simple harmonisations, and it seems almost redundant to notate them fully; but both this psalm and the preceding one, *Credidi*, appear like this. The other three psalms in the set are like the *Nisi Dominus*, a mix of homophony and simple polyphony.

4.4.2 The Hymns

There are six hymns in the manuscript: *Exultet cœlem laudibus* for St Matthew; two settings of *En prœclara virgo Clara*, the Vespers 2 hymn for St Clare; *Pange lingua gloriosi* for the feast of Corpus Christi; *Ave maris stella* for feasts of the BVM; and two that have many liturgical, paraliturgical, and extra-liturgical uses: *Veni Creator Spiritus* and the *Te Deum laudamus*. Like the psalms and Magnificats, these hymn settings are notated without the alternate chanted verses; they also represent a range of compositional types.

While *cantus firmus* composition is an older method than imitative polyphony, it remained current throughout the sixteenth century. The settings of *Exultet cœlem laudibus*, *Pange lingua gloriosi*, and one of the settings of *En prœclara virgo Clara* are *cantus firmus* settings of a single verse. The second setting of Clare's hymn and the *Veni Creator Spiritus* are also *cantus firmus* settings, but they set multiple verses – the *Veni Creator Spiritus* very simple, the *En prœclara* more complex. The first two polyphonic verses of the *Ave maris stella* are freely composed, but the third includes an elaboration of the hymn melody in the Tenor voice. These three multi-verse settings have separate 'Amen' sections; the *Veni Creator Spiritus* even has a second 'Amen' that has been added in red ink. The *Te Deum laudamus* is different again: it is, like many of the psalms, a simple rhythmicised harmonisation of a recitation tone. It begins based on the hymn's traditional melody but departs from it in a striking way, in what may be a uniquely Florentine practice.

En præclara virgo Clara seems to be a late addition to Clare's office: it does not appear in sources before the beginning of the fifteenth century (Boccali 2011, 129–30). Geographically, the closest source to Biffoli-Sostegni is Biblioteca Riccardiana codice 232, a late fifteenth-century Florentine source, where it is placed at the very end of the book, after two hymns for Clare and Francis that have the legend 'nuper editus', or 'newly composed'. Its melody is the hymn *Decus morum dux minorum*, an early hymn for Francis, from which it also takes its poetic form: each of the six verses ends with the first line of another older hymn; for instance, 'En præclara virgo Clara / regnat in regno luminum / quam amasti desponsasti / Jesu, corona virginum'. These resonances would remind the nuns of the interconnectedness of their worship, as they summon memories of the feasts of the virgin saints (*Jesu, corona virginum*), Ascension (*Jesu nostra redemptio*), Advent (*Conditor alme siderum*), the BVM (*O gloriosa Domina*), Francis (*In cælesti collegio*), and Pentecost (*Beata nobis gaudia*).

Using the *Ricordanze*, we can match the other hymns to the convent year with some confidence. The hymn for Matthew is clearly patronal; the *Pange lingua* would be useful for the annual visit of the Corpus Christi procession. The *Ave maris stella* could be used on any number of Marian feasts, but most particularly for the Immaculate Conception, one of San Matteo's most important liturgies. The simplicity of the *Veni Creator Spiritus* may reflect how often the hymn was used in the regular business of the convent: not only was it part of the liturgy of Pentecost, it also formed part of the ceremony for any official visit by a male priest or friar other than the confessor; it was sung at the election of the abbess, and at the vestition and profession of new nuns. The *Te Deum laudamus* was even more ubiquitous, for it was part of the weekly Divine Office, as well as being required for visitations and elections; the nuns of San Matteo would also sing it on 31 December (the feast of St Silvester) as part of their specific devotion (see Section 3.3.3).

The *Te Deum* is an unusually long hymn, with twenty-nine verses, and its melody is unusually complex. It starts relatively simply with a reciting tone in two halves, the first finishing on A, the second on G, but after several verses, it changes its tonal centre and has two longer complementary melodies that end on E. It is one of the oldest hymns in the liturgy, and it is remarkably stable over time and location: the *Te Deum* in medieval Italy is almost identical to the *Te Deum* in early modern England (Aplin 1979). Yet the setting in the Biffoli-Sostegni manuscript presents a different

Example/Audio 14a *Te Deum laudamus*, verse 1 compared: I-Fmsm MS 551 and B-Bc 27766. Audio file available at www.cambridge.org/stras

Example/Audio 14b *Te Deum laudamus*, verse 19 compared: I-Fmsm MS 551 and B-Bc 27766. Audio file available at www.cambridge.org/stras

approach: it uses the same melody throughout, always cadencing on A and G, until the very last verse which has three endings on G, A, and G. This simplification almost renders the hymn into song: at the very least, it becomes much easier to sing and remember. These two passages illustrate the difference, from the beginning of the chant (Example 14a/Audio 14a), and from after the traditional melody changes from one form to the next (Example 14b/Audio 14b): the top system gives the chant as rendered in a late fifteenth-century Clarissan manuscript from Florence, now in the Museo di San Marco (I-Fmsm), below the version in the Biffoli-Sostegni manuscript.

There are many polyphonic settings of the *Te Deum*, but only two others proceed in the same way as the Biffoli-Sostegni setting. Both are found in a contemporaneous manuscript from the Florentine Cathedral that appears to have been for the use of the boy choristers (see Section 4.6). There are traces of the *Te Deum* being used outside the Church in Florentine culture: it was sung by children in the streets as part of processions and even to conclude devotional plays (*sacre rappresentationi*), and it is included in fourteenth- and fifteenth-century collections of *laude* texts created for Florence's confraternities (Newbigin 1983, 290; Wilson 2001, 296). In one of these, the words are preceded by the instruction, 'to be sung in the manner of Piero di Mariano', indicating a specific mode of performance or melody that differs from the traditional chant.

4.4.3 The Office of St Clare

Of all the unusual music in the Biffoli-Sostegni manuscript, the twelve antiphons for the two Vespers of St Clare are perhaps the most startling (Clare is accorded a double feast in Franciscan worship, meaning the liturgy lasts for two days). They are unique, as the only known set of polyphonic Vespers antiphons in the sixteenth-century repertoire.[68] Eleven of them are copied together and appear to have been composed as a set. The twelfth, *Salve sponsa Dei*, the Magnificat antiphon for Vespers 2, is separated from the main set, physically and stylistically.

Apart from *Salve sponsa Dei*, the Clare Office items are composed in the early to mid sixteenth-century imitative style, in which the chant is rhythmically adapted and ornamented to fit the polyphonic fabric. They also display the specific characteristics of sixteenth-century equal-voice polyphony: increased and highlighted dissonances, and implied parallelisms, as in the opening breves of Antiphon 3 for Vespers 1, *Hæc in paternis laribus* (Example 15/Audio 15). The harmonic stasis created by imitative voices at the unison is less apparent here, as the chant melodies do not lend themselves to this kind of treatment. All the antiphons belong to that subset of *voci pari* writing that does not automatically suggest a bass instrument in accompaniment of higher equal voices, since the Bassus crosses the other parts from time to time.

---

[68] Alejandro Planchart posited that Guillaume DuFay composed full sets for St Francis and St Anthony of Padua, but they do not survive (Planchart 2006). Two fifteenth-century manuscripts in the Biblioteca Capitolare in Verona, MSS 758 and 759, contain two different polyphonic settings of four psalm antiphons and the Magnificat antiphon for the feast of St Lucy. It is possible they were owned by the convent of Santa Lucia in Verona (Stras 2024).

Example/Audio 15 B-Bc 27766, 97v–98r: *Hæc in paternis laribus*, bb. 1–16.
Audio file available at www.cambridge.org/stras

The rhymed Office of St Clare was composed in the thirteenth century by Julius of Speyer, using the melodies and poetic structure of his Office of St Francis and occasionally echoing its text (Baroffio and Kim 2004). Typically for rhymed offices, the melodies are arranged in a rising modal sequence: for Vespers 1, the psalm antiphons are in Modes 1–5 and the Magnificat antiphon in Mode 6; for Vespers 2, the psalm antiphons are in Modes 2–6 and the Magnificat antiphon returns to Mode 2. In all but one case – the Magnificat antiphon for Vespers 1 *Duce cælesti numine* – the Biffoli-Sostegni polyphony uses the original melodies. The Biffoli-Sostegni setting of *Duce cælesti numine* uses a melody in Mode 1, albeit one that is still taken from the liturgy of St Francis: the Biffoli-Sostegni setting may indicate a local variation of the Office.[69]

Whereas the psalm antiphons and the Magnificat antiphon for Vespers 1 share a high cleffing disposition – three treble clefs and a soprano clef ($g_2g_2g_2c_1$) – the

---

[69] This is the melody that now appears in the *Cantuale Romano-Seraphicum* (Bruning 1951, 209). Its only early sources on www.cantusdatabase.org are Fribourg, Bibliothèque des Cordeliers, 2, and the Burns Antiphoner at Boston College, in which it sets a non-allocated antiphon for the feast of St Francis, *Plaude turba paupercula*.

Figure 9 B-Bc 27766, 59v–60r: *Salve sponsa Dei* (Bibliothèque du Conservatoire royal de Bruxelles).

Magnificat antiphon for Vespers 2, *Salve sponsa Dei,* is in low clefs ($c_4c_4F_3F_4$). *Salve sponsa Dei* is unlike any other work in the manuscript, both visually and aurally. It is written in black chant notation in all four parts, and since chant is always notated in low clefs, this may account for the clef configuration (Figure 9). Because the antiphon melody has a range of over an octave, all the other voices necessarily must cross it – and each other – in an almost continuous progression of parallel sonorities (Example 16/Audio 16). The melody generated by the crossing voices is not reflected on the page: it is a melody of community, not individuality. Even within the characteristics of *voci pari* polyphony, this setting pushes the boundaries, creating something that is wholly foreign to both the nuns' usual soundworld and the sound of sixteenth-century polyphony more broadly.

Salve sponsa Dei is not copied with the rest of the Clare Office; instead, it appears in a correctly ordered sequence with the Vespers psalms for the Common of Virgins and the BVM, one of the *En præclara virgo Clara* settings, and a Magnificat. This suggests that these two sets are distinct: it is unlikely that the polyphonic psalms and the polyphonic antiphons would have been used in the same liturgical event. It is curious that the eleven antiphons, so clearly composed as a unit, do not include a setting of *Salve sponsa Dei*; perhaps the polyphonic chant setting existed already in the convent, and was used in preference to a new composition.

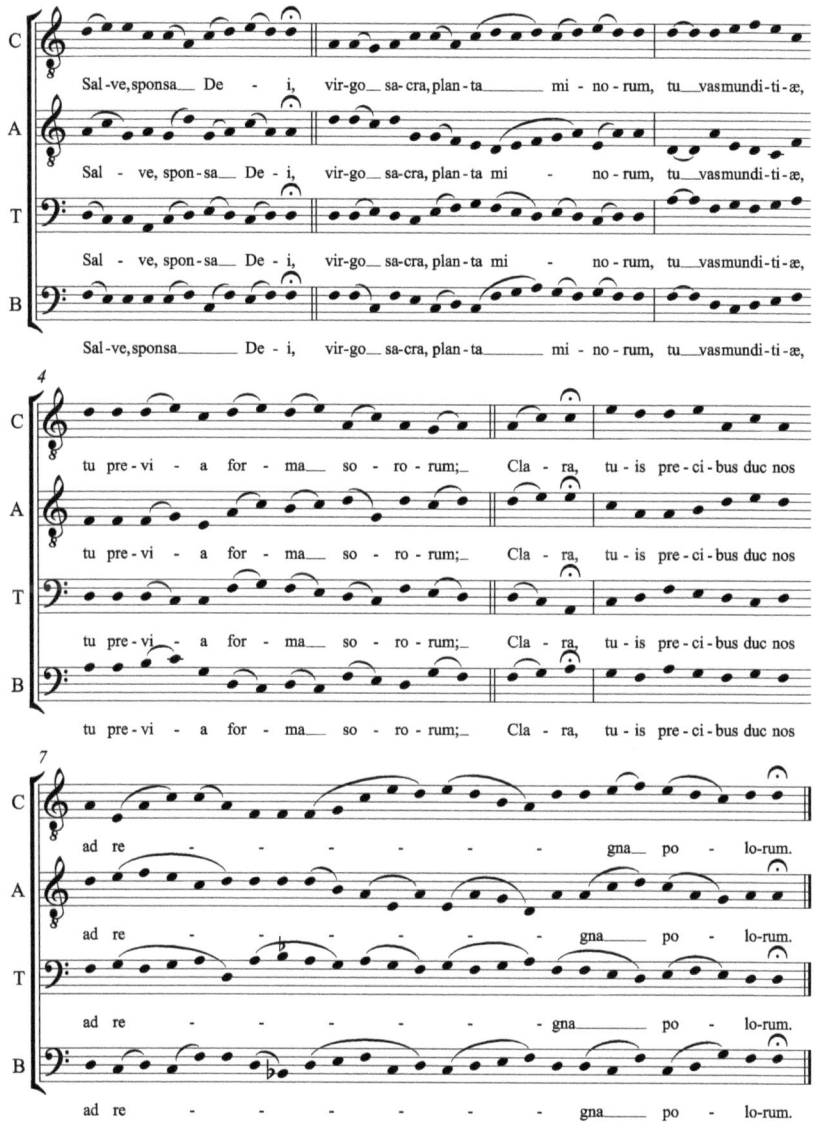

Example/Audio 16 B-Bc 27766, 59v–60r: *Salve sponsa Dei*.
Audio file available at www.cambridge.org/stras

The antiphons might also have been useful in another scenario, as a dramatic centrepiece to the convent's celebration – a musical *sacra rappresentazione* of the order's origin story. The whole sequence tells of Clare's childhood devotion to Francis and her decision to enter religious life; her sister Agnes, who witnesses Clare's death; and their reunion in Heaven. *Salve sponsa Dei*, the Magnificat antiphon that was the highlight of the two-day feast, describes Clare's leadership and her founding of the Clarissans' spiritual family. While they sang about the meaning of vocation for female religious, the nuns might also have reflected on the relationships between Clare and Agnes. How poignant for Suor Agnoleta, whose sister Caterina followed her into San Matteo – and all the pairs of sisters admitted to the convent over the next hundred years – to sing of a sister's love, not just with her blood kin but also with her sisters in Christ.

4.4.4 The Lenten Sequence

There is another shorter sequence of works, copied contiguously in the manuscript, that suggests some form of paraliturgical devotion rather than liturgical celebration. Four motets setting texts from Lenten offices – three responsory verses and one antiphon – seem incongruous, as Lent is usually a period of abstinence and enclosure. That being said, the *Ricordanze* does occasionally record extra expenses for food for the second Sunday of Lent, so perhaps San Matteo's community were not wholly abstemious or retiring, or perhaps the sequence was used during Carnival.

While settings of Magnificat antiphons can easily be directly incorporated into liturgical worship, the same is not true of settings of some other kinds of office texts: the feast or day to which they belong is sometimes more important than their place in the liturgy. Motets based on office texts might have been sung during/over Low Masses (see Section 3.1), or in a less formal devotional setting. These four settings are unlikely to have been used at Matins, and they are not in liturgical order. Nevertheless, they create a didactic narrative structure (invocation – action – problem – resolution) that explains the deprivation of Lent, perhaps to placate any frustration or dissent with a plea for patience:

1. *Venite benedicti patris mei* percipite regnum quod vobis paratum est ab origine mundi ('Come, you blessed of My Father, receive the Kingdom, which was prepared for you from the foundation of the world'). (Responsory verse, First Tuesday of Lent)
2. *Jesus autem cum jejunasset* quadraginta diebus et quadraginta noctibus postea esuriit ('Thus Jesus, with fasting for forty days and forty nights, became hungry'). (Antiphon, First Sunday of Lent)
3. *Multiplicati sunt qui tribulant me* et dicunt non est salus illi in deo ejus exsurge domine salvum me fac deus meus ('They are many who trouble me and say: There is no salvation for him in his God. Arise, O Lord, make me safe, My God'). (Responsory verse, Passion Sunday)
4. *Ecce nunc tempus acceptabile* ecce nunc dies salutis commendemus nosmetipsos in multa patientia ('Behold, now is the acceptable time: behold, now is

the day of salvation. Therefore, in these days let us commend ourselves to much patience'). (Responsory verse, First Sunday of Lent)

The *Ricordanze* notes that every year, as Lent was ending, the convent hosted friars who would sing the Passion (see Section 3.2). At the very end of the manuscript, written by a different scribe to the rest in an informal way, is the choir's response from the *Improperia*, or the Reproaches, for Good Friday.

4.5 Motets for Other Feasts and Celebrations

The selection of texts that make up the rest of the manuscript corresponds with more of the convent's most important feasts and celebrations. While some of these motets have an origin in liturgical chant, they could be used throughout the year in other contexts. For instance, the short antiphon *Da pacem, Domine* belongs liturgically to the Summer Histories 'de Machabæis'; between Pentecost and Advent, stories from the Old Testament were read during the Divine Office. However, the antiphon became used as a general exhortation for peace throughout the year – and no doubt, the story of the Judas Maccabaeus and his struggle against Imperial Rome resonated strongly with the Florentine Republic.[70]

Another antiphon that would have been used at least as frequently out of liturgical context as within is *Veni sponsa Christi*, the Magnificat antiphon for the Common of Virgins. It had a central position in the vestition ceremony, when a girl was formally received as a novice. It might be said or sung as the girl is embraced by the abbess, after she had been sprinkled with holy water, and before she is led into enclosure.[71] Some sources specify that the abbess or the cantrix should begin the chant, and the choir continue, finishing with an 'Alleluia' (Aulisio 1595, 2:*** 3, 29). This appears to be what is indicated in the Biffoli-Sostegni manuscript: the chant incipit is given on the top stave, then the rest of the chant given in black notation. The other three voices are notated in white mensural notation. As brief as it is, it still leans into the dissonances of equal-voice imitation, perhaps with a touch of mischief as it introduces an unprepared dissonance on the word 'præparavit' (Example 17/Audio 17). The special place of this motet in the convent's repertoire is sweetly indicated by a rebus that substitutes a small crown for the word 'coronam' in the index.

Sometimes there is an element of adaptation in the texts that takes them out of the liturgy, perhaps reflecting a local practice. The four-section litany, called *Kyrie eleison* in the index, is the briefest of *litaniæ breves*; while it might be

---

[70] Compare the modest settings in Vatican CS 15 (Rodin 2012, 174–76, 328–35).
[71] A 1571 *ordo* from a Clarissan convent in Padua, British Library Additional MS 14078, shows the antiphon was used in both vestition and profession rites at that convent.

Example/Audio 17 B-Bc 27766, 88v–89r: *Veni sponsa Christi*.
Audio file available at www.cambridge.org/stras

a choral opening that is intended to be followed by chant, its invocations do not follow the opening pattern of any printed litany. The Magnificat antiphon for Vespers 2 for St Francis, *Salve sancte pater*, has interpolated text at the beginning and the end which would make it liturgically invalid yet suitable as an invocation, perhaps during a devotion specific to the Franciscan orders. The motet *Inter natos mulierum* uses fragments of a Matins responsory and verse for St John the Baptist and adds an 'Alleluia' at the end of its two short parts. While Alleluias have a specific liturgical place in the Mass and during the Office at particular times of year, they can also function as a musical refrain in paraliturgical or spiritual works. Here, they lend gravitas to an otherwise simple setting, potentially intended to ornament worship on the feast of the saint, one of Florence's protectors (the baptistry is dedicated to San Giovanni Battista, the cathedral to Santa Maria del Fiore, the city's other patron).

4.5.1 Music for the Blessed Virgin Mary

As might be expected, there is a strong concentration of Marian texts: fourteen works, eighteen percent of the manuscript's total. These may be associated with a particular feast – the Annunciation, Assumption, Nativity, or Immaculate Conception – but often they are interchangeable or assigned to multiple feasts. This group contains the most complex music in the manuscript (apart from the masses); and – perhaps not coincidentally – seven of the nine works that are attributed to a named composer, either in the manuscript or elsewhere (including Adriano Willaert, Costanzo Festa, and Jean Mouton/Pierre Moulu; See Appendix A). It also contains the oldest – Loyset Compère's (c. 1445–1518) *Paranymphus salutatet virginem* – and the newest works.

These attributed pieces may have been assimilated into the convent's repertoire through other sources, but the two settings of *Sancta Maria succurre miseris*, the Magnificat antiphon for feasts of the BVM, look to have been composed explicitly for nuns, perhaps even for the nuns of San Matteo. One is by Antonio Moro, the copyist of the manuscript, the other by Francesco Bocchini, the *maestro di cappella* at the cathedral of Pisa. The text of *Sancta Maria succurre miseris* contains a reference to nuns' communities: 'Pray for the people, intervene for the clergy, intercede for women consecrated to God' ('Ora pro populo, intervene pro clero, intercede pro devoto femineo sexu'). The two composers respond to the phrase 'intercede pro devoto femineo sexu' in different ways, which nonetheless both signal its significance for nuns: Moro with a chromatic inflection on the word 'femineo'; Bocchini by making the passage longer, with more repetitions, than his treatment of the 'populo' and the 'clero' (Stras 2017a, 210–12).[72]

Only two of the four Marian antiphons for Compline are included in the manuscript: *Ave Regina cælorum*, which was sung from the Purification of Mary (2 February) to Maundy Thursday, and *Salve Regina*, which was sung from the Octave of Pentecost to the beginning of Advent; *Alma Redemptoris*

---

[72] For another slightly earlier motet that uses both these techniques to set these words, attributed to Suor Leonora d'Este, see (Stras 2017b, 650–55).

mater, for Advent to the Purification, and *Regina cœli*, for Easter to Pentecost, are missing. The *alternatim* setting of *Salve Regina* is one of the most striking in the manuscript. The practice of setting the *Salve Regina* in alternating polyphony and chant dated at least as far back as the fifteenth century, but this setting's style is more congruent with the first half of the sixteenth century in terms of its advanced imitative writing. Although it is written in a three-plus-one disposition – the top three voices sharing the same range, the Bassus a fifth lower – it manages to avoid the trademark sounding parallel intervals of *voci pari* writing. Yet it also sometimes inverts the expectations of its disposition: often two or three voices will be in extended canon, and unusually this can feature the Bassus acting with two of the higher voices – creating a one-plus-three texture with the highest voice as a descant. Overlapping and frequent dissonances create a restless mood, which contrasts sharply with moments of stark homophony.

The *Sancta Maria, letaniæ della Madonna* is another curious piece that may have a local resonance. The *cantus firmus* is the usual litany chant, familiar to modern audiences through Claudio Monteverdi's *Sonata sopra Sancta Maria*, but it is not stable, moving between the Cantus, Altus, and Bassus. It departs from the *cantus firmus* at the fourth invocation, 'Sancta mater apostolorum', and the fifth invocation invents a new title for the BVM, 'Sancta mater navigantum' (Holy Mother of the seafarers). This reference to sailors seems incongruous for a landlocked convent, yet undoubtedly every nun's family was to a greater or lesser extent reliant on maritime trade, and Florence's merchant and military fleet was growing. In January 1560, Cosimo I de' Medici petitioned the pope for permission to create a new naval chivalric Order, the Cavalieri di Santo Stefano, which was granted in 1561 (Gemignani 2002, 169–74). The order had its headquarters in Pisa, and its establishment was celebrated in grand fashion at the cathedral in 1562, where Francesco Bocchini was *maestro di cappella*.

4.5.2 Music Appropriate for the Convent 'Visits'

Not all the Marian music is technically challenging. The miniature *Sancta Dei genitrix* begins as canon on the unison then moves lightly through homophony and imitation. Like so many pieces in the manuscript, one voice – here the Tenor – bears the chant melody, which is given a rhythm that allows for imitation, for instance, at the words 'ad Dominum' (Example 18/Audio 18).

The *Constituzioni* refers to a practice of regular 'visits', which involved the whole convent gathering in front of a particular altar – the Crucifix, the BVM, and the Nativity – and singing (see Section 3.3). While there is no specific record of these devotions happening in the sixteenth century at San Matteo,

Example/Audio 18 B-Bc 27766, 46v–47r: *Sancta Dei genitrix*.
Audio file available at www.cambridge.org/stras

similar practices elsewhere are documented contemporaneously (Stras 2018, 297). There are several works, including the *Sancta Dei genitrix*, that would be suited to this type of collective musical activity, some simple enough to be learned by those who did not read music. Almost all the motets could also be used either as part of the liturgy or alongside it, but they highlight the blurred lines, or the continuum, between the materials for formal and informal worship in the relatively closed and cyclical culture of the convent.

Two motets for the Cross are in three voices; a third is in four voices. The simplest of the three remains homophonic throughout: a three-voice setting of *Adoramus te Christe*, an antiphon for the Feasts of the Invention and the Exaltation of the Cross. The three-voice *O crux splendidior* is longer and more adventurous, perhaps even more secular, with strings of suspensions, affective phrasing, and a hexachordal pun on 'sola' ('sol-la') that might please the musically literate (Example 19/Audio 19).

Example/Audio 19 B-Bc 27766, 153v–154r: *O crux splendidior*, bb. 14–42. Audio file available at www.cambridge.org/stras

The four-voice motet also sets the text *Adoramus te Christe* but pairs it with the opening of St Gregory's prayer for Good Friday, *Domine Jesu Christe*, and the third part of the Sanctus of the Mass Ordinary, the Benedictus. It is the only motet in the manuscript that is a *cento*, or patchwork, text, and its composition is also a patchwork of *falsobordone*, imitation, and canon. Although one of the manuscript's simpler works, it is nonetheless an impressive contribution to the convent's sonic identity (see Video 1).

There is only one liturgical text for Christmas in the manuscript – *Hodie Christus natus est*, the Magnificat antiphon for the Octave of Christmas – in a mostly homophonic and straightforward setting. There are, however, three settings of the carol *Verbum caro factum est*, two in three voices and one in four. The two three-voice versions set the refrain and only one verse of the carol. They have the same melody and are both notated in high clefs: the additional voices weave around each other in imitation, but without any specific reference to the melody.

The four-voice version is also in high clefs, but it is considerably more complex. It has two settings of the refrain, one at the beginning and the other at the end: these are in duple time, contrasting with the natural triple of the traditional melody. Its three verses adopt different strategies: the first is in four voices, with the carol as a cantus firmus; the second is a trio, fully imitative but using fragments of the melody for its material; the third is a duo, with one voice singing the carol, but there is an optional *si placet* third voice, with the instruction, 'questa parte si canta piacendovi quando sieno cantate e'l duo' ('this part can be sung when you sing the duo, if you wish'). The most surprising moments in the motet come at the cadences in the refrains, when the Tenor carries on with a curious ornament, raising the fifth of the chord by a semitone (Example 20/Audio 20).

4.5.3 The Italian Songs

There are three settings of vernacular spiritual texts – a *canzona* by Petrarch, a *barzelletta* first published in 1503 (da Cingoli 1503), and an anonymous four-stanza text in blank verse (*versi sciolti*). They might have been used for private devotion, but the blank verse suggests a dramatic context, perhaps a remnant of a *sacra rappresentatione*. The musical style of all three resembles the early Florentine madrigal of the 1520s and 30s, including those provided by Philippe Verdelot for Niccolò Machiavelli's plays (Cummings 2004, 143–50). There are many contemporary settings of Petrarch's *Vergine bella*, but few as simple and unprepossessing as the one here: it is in four voices with the upper two voices sharing the same range. The text is declaimed succinctly and without ornament; the structure is compact. In contrast, the *barzelletta* setting, *Non è di alcun di*

Example/Audio 20 B-Bc 27766, 64v–65r: *Verbum caro factum est*, bb. 1–10.
Audio file available at www.cambridge.org/stras

gloria degno, is much more mannered. Although the text extols the virtues of virginity, the setting uses similar affective gestures to the setting of *O crux splendidior*: the chains of suspensions, and the delayed voice introducing the cadential ornament (Example 21/Audio 21). The blank verse, *Giesù benign' e pio*, is a Eucharistic poem: the four stanzas are set to two musical parts, verses 1 and 3 to the first part, verses 2 and 4 to the second. Because the setting is almost uniformly homophonic, it is very possible to view it as a solo song, perhaps with lute or keyboard accompaniment.

4.6 Reflections on the Music of the Biffoli-Sostegni Manuscript

The Biffoli-Sostegni manuscript contains many anonymous works, alongside ones by local composers and a more disparate repertoire in terms of time and place, showing that the owners, however confined by vows of stability, were in touch with layers of musical activity beyond their walls. The repertoire dates from potentially the last decades of the fifteenth century to that contemporaneous with

Example/Audio 21 B-Bc 27766, 130v–131r: *Non è di alcun di gloria degno*, bb. 25–38. Audio file available at www.cambridge.org/stras

its copying in 1560, and its sheer range of genres makes a blanket summary of its compositional style impossible. Nonetheless, there are ways to suggest coherence in some of its repertoire, through surface characteristics to technical elements. The similarities in gestures between *O crux splendidior* and *Non è di alcun di gloria degno* are a case in point: while we cannot claim that the two pieces were written by the same composer, they may have been gathered into the manuscript because of the recipients' response to their affect. And there is a cadential 'signature' that also appears in several works – the raised fifth that is so surprising in the four-voice setting of *Verbum caro factum est* also appears in the *Messa sopra Je le lerray*, and the short *Sancta Dei genetrix* (compare Example 18 and Example 20).

At least some of the many anonymous settings in the manuscript may have been composed by one of the nuns. Some have minor errors in the contrapuntal writing, which may suggest that their composers were untroubled by the occasional transgression, but the relative simplicity of some settings does not necessarily imply inexperience. Florence's convents housed many creative women who excelled in art, music, and poetry. Florentine musical tastes, particularly in respect of sacred music, inclined to the austere, with cleanly enunciated text and a modest approach to harmonic or affective ornament (D'Accone 1983).

There are direct correspondences between the music in the manuscript and other contemporary Florentine sources. The three-voice *Verbum caro factum est* settings share the Cantus line with the three-voice setting of the carol in the *Primo libro de laude spirituali*, published by Serafino Razzi in 1563, and dedicated to Caterina de' Ricci, the (eventually canonised) abbess of San Vincenzo in Prato. There are also a few intriguing similarities with the repertoire in a manuscript for the Florentine Duomo, Archivio musicale dell'Opera di Santa Maria del Fiore, MS II-13.

MS II-13 is presumed to have been copied in the 1540s. After years of inactivity caused by plague and political unrest, the cathedral's musical institution was re-established soon after Cosimo I de' Medici was installed as Duke of Tuscany in 1537. MS II-13 has some unusual features that suggest it was compiled for the new boy choristers: a single hymn tune setting is copied out multiple times with the texts of different hymns, and the underlay of the words under the music throughout is extremely careful, with almost no use of the usual 'ditto' sign ('ij'), making it more practical for inexperienced musicians who would not be able to place the words intuitively to the music. The hymns do not correspond precisely with the Duomo's calendar; rather, they include hymns for the patronal feasts of Florence's four boys' confraternities: Saint Raphael, Saint John the Baptist, Saint Nicholas, and the Purification of the BVM. But the manuscript also has four important links to the Biffoli-Sostegni manuscript. First, its setting of *Hodie Christus natus est* is identical to that in the nuns' book. Second, MS II-13 also contains psalms that, like the *In convertendo* of Biffoli-Sostegni, are notated in only breves and semibreves in harmonisations that could be extemporised without notation by experienced singers. Third, it contains two settings of the *Te Deum laudamus* that, like the Biffoli-Sostegni setting, use only the first part of the chant melody; these two settings are also substantially alike.

Finally, both manuscripts contain settings of the text *Ecce quam bonum et quam iucundum*. While ostensibly a familiar text from the liturgy, with many uses from a responsory at Matins to a gradual during Mass, the song had a very specific meaning to Florentines, as it had been the cherished anthem of the followers of Girolamo Savonarola. The Duomo setting is a refrain to a number of feast-specific verses (Corpus Christi, Holy Week, etc) that suggest a Eucharistic function (Giacomelli 2001, 395–98); the Biffoli-Sostegni setting is of just the refrain, in which the melody is shared by Cantus and Altus (Example 22/Audio 22). It seems incongruous in a manuscript for a Clarissan

Music at a Florentine Convent

Example/Audio 22 B-Bc 27766, 87v–88r: *Ecce quam bonum*.
Audio file available at www.cambridge.org/stras

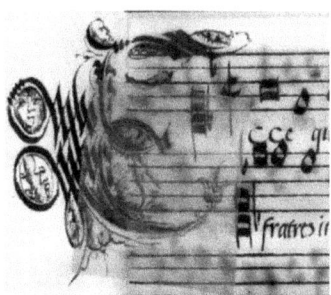

Figure 10 B-Bc 27766, 87v: *Ecce quam bonum*, Tenor, portrait of Savonarola (Bibliothèque du Conservatoire royal de Bruxelles).

convent, given the enmity that existed between the Franciscans and Savonarola's Dominican followers, but it is not easily dismissed as a neutral expression of communal goodwill. Tucked in the initial E in the Tenor voice is a tiny but unmistakeable portrait of Savonarola (Figure 10). Its presence is inexplicable, except perhaps as another reminder of how Florence's history and its musical culture resounded in even its most secluded corners.

5 Conclusion

The sounding of music was a powerful and hugely important element of convent life. The music manuscript so beautifully presented to Suor Agnoleta Biffoli and Suor Clemenzia Sostegni in 1560 may still have been in the convent in 1614, when the Galilei sisters were given the white novitiate's veil. The *Ricordanze* shows how circular the convent's economy was, even in the sixteenth century: a dead nun's 'belongings' reverted to the household, and those that had domestic use, such as blankets, mattresses, or small items of furniture, could be 'purchased' by the sisters, either for themselves or for their *discepole*, from the allowance given to them by the convent; other items could be sold outside the convent. While the Biffoli-Sostegni manuscript would technically have become common property the minute it entered San Matteo, we cannot say for certain how long it remained there after Suor Clemenzia's death. Nevertheless, a book of polyphony for worship and devotion would have been intrinsically useful, particularly given the strictures on newer styles of music laid out in the archbishop's *Trattato*; and we might wonder whether there would have been either a market for its very specific repertoire or a desire on behalf of the abbess or sacristan to relinquish it.

Moreover, the liturgical needs of the convent would have changed very little, if at all: Just as they would have done for Suor Agnoleta and Suor Clemenzia, the nuns of San Matteo would have escorted Suor Maria Celeste and Suor Arcangela singing *Veni Creator Spiritus*; after they had been anointed, their new family would have joined them in singing *Veni sponsa Christi*, embraced them, and led them into the church, finishing with the *Te Deum laudamus*. Eventually, they would know entire sections of the liturgy by heart, and they would sing the psalms, hymns, and antiphons as if they were second nature. Even polyphony might be memorised, but a convent choirbook might have an additional role in forging communal bonds: since all the parts are copied on to a single opening of the book, the singers must stand close together, perhaps even touching, all eyes focussed on one source as they raise their voices in collective worship (Video 1).

Alexa Sand noted of medieval women's devotional books, 'If the women pictured are at once the women imagined to be looking at the page and the women who wrote and illustrated it, then the reflexive qualities of the image are

Video 1 B-Bc 27766, 84v–85r: *Adoramus te, Christe/Domine, Jesu Christe.*
www.cambridge.org/stras

multiplied, as in a hall of mirrors' (Sand 2014, 116). The Biffoli-Sostegni manuscript adds sound and echo to reflected colour and light; even if was no longer used for worship, its music, words, and images would have had value to the nuns, as prompts to reflect on their community, their daily recitation of the Divine Office and its meaning as God's work. The tiny nuns' faces that peer from the letters, recalling the generations that came before; the hymn texts left partial that required the memory to fill in the missing verses; the familiar words that would instantly summon a melody: all these reminders feed into the imagination of the reader even before a note is sung, making the manuscript not just an object for performance, but also a record of San Matteo's, and all its sisters', history.

Appendix A: Manuscript Contents

Table A.1(a) Manuscript contents, items 1–23

	Pages	Title	Disposition	Feast
1	1v–14r	Messa sopra Recordare Virgo Mater	$c_1c_1c_1c_2$	Mass Ordinary
2	14v–16r	Recordare Virgo Mater / Et ut advertas [attr. Josquin Desprez]	$c_1c_1c_1c_2$	Mass Offertory + prosa, Immaculate Conception of BVM
3	16v–18r	Dixit Dominus Domino meo	$c_1c_2c_2c_4$	Psalm, Vespers 1, Common of Saints
4	18v–21r	Confitebor tibi, Domine	$c_1c_2c_2c_4$	Psalm, Vespers 1, Common of Saints
5	21v–26r	Beatus vir qui timet Dominum	$c_1c_2c_3F_3$	Psalm, Vespers 1, Common of Saints
6	26v–29r	Laudate pueri Dominum	$c_3c_3c_3c_4$	Psalm, Vespers 1, Common of Saints
7	29v–30r	Laudate Dominum	$c_1c_2c_2c_4$	Psalm, Vespers 1, Common of Saints
8	30r–33	Exultet cœlum laudibus	$c_3c_4c_4F_4$	Hymn, Common of Apostles
9	33v–36r	Magnificat anima mea [primo tono]	$c_2c_2c_2c_4$	Magnificat, Vespers
10	36v–40r	Te Deum laudamus	$c_1c_3c_3F_3$	Hymn, Matins
11	40v–41r	Pange lingua gloriosi	$c_2c_3c_3F_3$	Vespers hymn, Corpus Christi
12	41v–43r	Sancta Maria succurre – Sre Antonio	$c_1c_1c_1c_3$	Magnificat antiphon, Commons of BVM

Table A.1(a) (cont.)

	Pages	Title	Disposition	Feast
13	43v–44r	*Vidi speciosam*	$c_4c_4c_4F_4$	Lauds/Vespers 2 antiphon, Assumption/Nativity of BVM, Common of Virgins
14	44v–46r	*Sancta Maria succurre* – Bocchini	$g_2g_2c_1c_1$	Magnificat antiphon, Commons of BVM
15	46v–47r	*Sancta Dei genitrix*	$c_3c_3c_3c_4$	Antiphon, Assumption of BVM
16	47v–48r	*Dixit Dominus Domino meo*	$c_2c_2c_3c_4$	Vespers psalms, Commons of BVM and of Virgins
17	48v–49r	*Laudate pueri Dominum*	$c_1c_1c_2c_3$	Vespers psalms, Commons of BVM and of Virgins
18	49v–50r	*Lætatus sum*	$c_1c_2c_3c_4$	Vespers psalms, Commons of BVM and of Virgins
19	50v–51r	*Nisi Dominus*	$c_1c_1c_1c_3$	Vespers psalms, Commons of BVM and of Virgins
20	51v–53r	*Lauda, Jerusalem*	$c_1c_1c_2c_3$	Vespers psalms, Commons of BVM and of Virgins
21	53v–55r	*En præclara virgo Clara*	$c_3c_4c_4F_4$	Hymn, Vespers 2, Clare
22	55v–59r	*Magnificat anima mea* [ottavo tono]	$g_2g_2c_1c_3$	Magnificat, Vespers
23	59v–60r	*Salve sponsa Dei*	$c_4c_4F_3F_4$	Magnificat antiphon, Vespers 2, Clare

Table A.1(b) Manuscript contents, items 24–45

	Pages	Title	Disposition	Feast
24	60v–61r	Da pacem Domine in diebus nostris	$c_3c_3c_3c_4$	Antiphon, suffrage for peace
25	61v–62r	En præclara virgo Clara	$c_4c_4F_4F_4$	Hymn, Vespers 2, Clare
26	62v–64r	In illo tempore: Thomas / Nisi videro – Bocchini	$c_1c_2c_2c_3$	Gospel, Octave of Easter
27	64v–67r	Verbum caro factum est I	$g_2g_2c_1c_3$	lauda, Christmas
28	67v–69r	Quam pulcra es amica mea [Jean Mouton or Pierre Moulu]	$c_4c_4c_4F_4$	Antiphon, Assumption/ Nativity BVM
29	69v–70r	Paranymphus salutat virginem – [Loyset Compère]	$F_3F_3F_4F_4$	Sequence, Annunciation BVM
30	70v–72r	Portas cœli aperuit Dominus / Hic est panis	$c_1c_3c_3F_4$	Eucharist [Combined text: Offertory, Thursday after Easter; Mass antiphon, Corpus Christi]
31	72v–73r	Hodie Christus natus est hodie salvator	$c_3c_3c_4F_3$	Magnificat antiphon, Octave of Christmas
32	73v–74r	Venite benedicti patris mei	$c_4c_4c_4F_4$	Antiphon, First Tuesday of Lent
33	74v–75r	Jesus autem cum jejunasset	$c_4c_4c_4F_4$	Antiphon, First Sunday and First Friday of Lent
34	75v–76r	Multiplicati sunt qui tribulant me	$c_4c_4c_4F_4$	Responsory, Fourth Saturday of Lent, Passion Sunday

Table A.1(b) (cont.)

	Pages	Title	Disposition	Feast
35	76v–77r	*Ecce nunc tempus*	$c_4c_4c_4F_4$	Magnificat antiphon, First Sunday of Lent
36	77v–80r	*Ave maris stella*	$c_3c_3c_3c_4$	Vespers hymn, Common of BVM [Conception]
37	80v–82r	*Veni Creator Spiritus*	$c_1c_1c_1c_3$	Hymn, Pentecost
38	82v–84r	*Vergine bella che di sol vestita*	$c_3c_3c_3F_3$	Madrigal (canzona)
39	84v–85r	*Adoramus te Christe / Domine Jesu Christe*	$c_3c_3c_3F_4$	Antiphon, Invention, and Exaltation of the Cross/Good Friday
40	85v–86r	*Inter natos mulierum*	$c_3c_3c_4F_3$	Responsory and verse, John the Baptist
41	86v–87r	*Hodie visitata est, a 3*	$c_1c_1c_3$	Antiphon, Annunciation of the BVM
42	87v–88r	*Ecce quam bonum*	$c_1c_1c_1c_3$	lauda
43	88v–89r	*Veni sponsa Christi*	$c_4c_4c_4c_4$	Magnificat antiphon, Common of Virgins; vestition/profession
44	89v–91r	*Hæc dies quam fecit*	$c_2c_2c_3c_4$	Gradual, Easter Sunday
45	91v–92r	*Sancta Maria, letaniæ della Madonna*	$c_1c_2c_3F_3$	Litany of the BVM

Table A.1(c) Manuscript contents, items 46–71

	Pages	Title	Disposition	Feast
46	92v–95r	Ave Maria gratia plena [Adriano Willaert]	$c_1c_2c_3c_4$	Antiphon, Advent and Christmas; Feasts of BVM
47	95v–96r	Iam sanctæ Claræ	$g_2g_2g_2c_1$	Antiphon, Vespers 1, Clare
48	96v–97r	Mundi totius gloriam	$g_2g_2g_2c_1$	Antiphon, Vespers 1, Clare
49	97v–98r	Hæc in paternis laribus puella	$g_2g_2g_2c_1$	Antiphon, Vespers 1, Clare
50	98v–99r	Sacra spirat infantia	$g_2g_2g_2c_1$	Antiphon, Vespers 1, Clare
51	99v–100r	Hanc et papa Gregorius fovit	$g_2g_2g_2c_1$	Antiphon, Vespers 1, Clare
52	100v–101r	Duce cælesti numine	$g_2g_2g_2c_1$	Magnificat antiphon, Vespers 1, Clare
53	101v–102r	Post vitæ Claræ terminum	$g_2g_2g_2c_1$	Antiphon, Vespers 2, Clare
54	102v–103r	Agnes ad agni nuptias	$g_2g_2g_2c_1$	Antiphon, Vespers 2, Clare
55	103v–104r	Sicut sorore prævia	$g_2g_2g_2c_1$	Antiphon, Vespers 2, Clare
56	104v–105r	Honorat Christi dextera	$g_2g_2g_2c_1$	Antiphon, Vespers 2, Clare
57	105v–106r	Laudans laudare studeat	$g_2g_2g_2c_1$	Antiphon, Vespers 2, Clare
58	106v–107r	Kyrie eleison. Sancta Maria	$c_1c_4c_4F_4$	Litany of the Saints
59	107v–109r	Dixit Dominus	$c_2c_2c_3c_4$	Psalm, Vespers 2, Common of Saints
60	109v–111r	Laudate pueri Dominum	$c_2c_2c_3c_4$	Psalm, Vespers 2, Common of Saints
61	111v–113r	Credidi propter quod locutus sum	$c_1c_2c_3c_4$	Psalm, Vespers 2, Common of Saints

Appendix A: Manuscript Contents

Table A.1(c) (cont.)

	Pages	Title	Disposition	Feast
62	113v–113bis.	In convertendo Dominus	$c_1c_3c_3F_3$	Psalm, Vespers 2, Common of Saints
63	113bis.v–118r	Domine, probasti me	$c_1c_1c_3c_4$	Psalm, Vespers 2, Common of Saints
64	118v–124r	Magnificat anima mea [primo tono]	$c_2c_2c_3c_4$	Magnificat, Vespers
65	124v–127r	Salve Regina, vita dulcedo	$c_4c_4c_4F_4$	Antiphon, Easter to Advent, Compline
66	127v–129r	Giesù benign' et pio	$g_2c_1c_2c_3$	Madrigal (versi sciolti)
67	129v–131r	Non è alcun di gloria degno	$c_1c_1c_1c_3$	Madrigal (barzelletta)
68	135v–149r	Messa con tre voci [Messa sopra Je le lerray]	$c_3c_4F_3$	Mass Ordinary
69	149v–151r	In illo tempore: vidit Jesus / Et videntes pharisæi	$c_1c_1c_3$	Gospel, St Matthew
70	151v–152r	Salve sancte pater	$c_2c_3c_4$	Antiphon (modified), St Francis
71	152v–153r	Ave Regina cælorum	$c_4c_4F_4$	Antiphon, Purification to Holy Week, Compline

Table A.1(d) Manuscript contents, items 72–78

	Pages	Title	Disposition	Feast
72	153v–154r	*O crux splendidior*	$c_2c_2c_4$	Antiphon, Vespers 1, Invention and Exaltation of the Cross
73	154v–155r	*Adoramus te Christe*	$c_2c_2c_4$	Antiphon, Invention, and Exaltation of the Cross
74	155v–156r	*Verbum caro factum est II*	$c_1c_1c_1$	lauda, Christmas
75	156v–157r	*Verbum caro factum est III*	$c_1c_1c_2$	lauda, Christmas
76	157v–158r	*Quam pulcra es et decora* [Costanzo Festa]	$c_1c_1c_4$	Antiphon, Assumption/Nativity of BVM
77	158v–164r	*Magnificat primo tono* [Jehan de Billon]	$g_2g_2c_1$	Magnificat, Vespers
78	165v–166r	*Popule meus*	c_4F_4	Improperium, Good Friday

Appendix B: The Women of San Matteo

Table B.1(a) The women of San Matteo, 1519–1531 († death; * in serbanza/serbo)

	Name	Religious name	Family name	first recorded	entry age	last recorded
1	Maria Benedetta	Maria Benedetta	–	1519	–	1519
2	Lisabetta	Lisabetta	–	1520	–	1520
3	Maria di Nicholo da Castiglione	Maria	Castiglione	1521	–	1521
4	Nanina di Giovanni Hubertini	Nannina	Ubertini	1526	–	1526
5	Crementia de' Ghaetani	Clemenzia	Gaetani	1530	–	†1530
6	Francescha di Domenico Gennai	Francesca	Gennai	1530	–	†1530
7	Angelicha di Piero Salviati	Angelica	Salviati	1530	–	†1530
8	Piera de' Giardelli	Piera	Giardelli	1530	–	†1530
9	Lodovicha de' Charducci	Lodovica	Carducci	1530	–	†1530
10	Cosa, servigiale	Cosa	–	1530	–	†1530
11	Lucretia de' Ricci	Lucrezia	Ricci	1530	–	†1530
12	Camilla	Camilla	–	1530	–	†1530
13	Agniolletta de' Soldini	Angioletta	Soldini	1530	–	†1548
14	Alexandra di Giovanni Hubaldini	Alessandra	Baldini	1530	–	1564
15	Hipolita di Francescho Salsolini	Ippolita	Sassolini	1530	–	1583
16	Chiara di Filippo Rondinegli	Chiara	Rondinelli	1530	–	1530
17	Katerina d'Agniolo Anselmi	Caterina	Anselmi	1530	–	1583
18	Pippa	Pippa	–	1531	–	†1531
19	Dianora di Giulio Parigi	Dianora	Parigi	1531	–	†1552
20	Horsina di Ser Masetto Cennini	Orsina	Cennini	1531	–	†1579

Table B.1(b) The women of San Matteo, 1532–1536 († death; * in serbanza/serbo)

	Name	Religious name	Family name	first recorded	entry age	last recorded
21	Maddalena de' Buondelmonte	Maddalena	Buondelmonte	1532	–	†1541
22	Fimecta di Giovanni Baroncegli	Fiametta	Baroncelli	1532	–	1532
23	Barbera di Charlo di San Verdiano	Barbara	San Verdiano	1532	–	1532
24	Francescha di S. Giovanbattista da Terra Nova	Francesca	Terranova	1532	–	1532
25	Vangelista de Cavalcanti	Evangelista	Cavalcanti	1533	–	†1533
26	Figenia di Pier Dassole	Ephigenia	Da Sole	1533	–	1533
27	Diamante di David de' Ricci	Diamante	Ricci	1533	–	1585
28	Maria d'Allesandro Chavalchanti	Maria	Cavalcanti	1533	–	1583
29	Horecta d'Antonio Chanducci	Oretta	Canducci	1533	–	1591
30	Lodovicha di Simona Speciale	Lodovica	Speziale	1534	–	†1552
31	Margherita de' Buonaccorsi	Margherita	Buonaccorsi	1535	–	†1535
32	Apollonia de' Marci	Apollonia	Marci	1535	–	†1538
33	Laurenza de' Giardinelli	Lorenza	Giardinelli	1535	–	†1543
34	Firecta di Francescho Grifi	Fioretta	Grifi	1535	–	†1556
35	Ginevra di Giovanni di Iacceto	Ginevra	–	1535	–	1583
36	Laldomina di Giovanni Ghaetani	Laudomina	Gaetani	1535	–	1564
37	Archangiola de' Bartoli	Arcangela	Bartoli	1536	–	†1536
38	Ghostançia di Ghuaspar del Chaccia	Costanza	Del Caccia	1536	–	1536
39	Lucreçia di Mattio Rondinegli	Lucrezia	Rondinelli	1536	–	†1559

Table B.1(c) The women of San Matteo, 1538–1550 († death; * in serbanza/serbo)

	Name	Religious name	Family name	first recorded	entry age	last recorded
40	Maria Maddalena di Giovani Gualberto Cennini	Maria Maddalena	Cennini	1538	–	1583
41	Margerita di Pier Buonavolti	Margherita	Buonavolti	1539	–	1583
42	Massimilla d'Alexandro Scharlatti	Massimilla	Scarlatti	1539	–	1590
43	Violante di Lorenzo Tanini	Violante	Tanini	1540	–	†1552
44	Kamilla di Lorençio Tanini	Camilla	Tanini	1540	–	1583
45	Cremençia di Ruberto Sostegni	Clemenzia	Sostegni	1541	–	†1612
46	Maddalena di Giovanni di ser Pier Sini	Maddalena	Sini	1542	–	1619
47	Serafina di Giuliano del Seta	Serafina	Del Seta	1543	–	1583
48	Gismonda di Marco di Giovani Richasoli	Gismonda	Ricasoli	1544	–	1544
49	Bartholomea di Luigi Cennini	Bartolomea	Cennini	1545	–	1545
50	Antonia di Nicholo Mori	Antonia	Mori	1545	–	1583
51	Marietta di Giuliano Salvetti	Maria	Salvetti	1546	–	†1558
52	Maddalena di Francesco di Giovanni Ghaetani	Piera	Gaetani	1547	–	1599
53	Agnioletta di Francesco Biffoli	Agnoleta	Biffoli	1548	–	1608
54	Chaterina di Francesco di Giovanbattista Biffoli	Cassandra	Biffoli	1549	–	1608
55	Maria di Giovanni di Fran.co Chorsi	Arcangela	Corsi	1550	–	1583
56	Lisabetta di Franscesco Ghaetani	Lisabetta	Gaetani	1550	–	1583

Table B.1(d) The women of San Matteo, 1551–1559 († death; * in serbanza/serbo)

	Name	Religious name	Family name	first recorded	entry age	last recorded
57	Maddalena di Domenico Ghiudetti	Cherubina	Giudetti	1551	–	1583
58	Felice di Agniolo di Caro Fortunati	Felice	Fortunati	1551	–	1583
59	Mattea	Mattea	–	1551	–	1558
60	Lexandra di Nicholo Buondelmonti	Lorenza	Buondelmonte	1553	–	1553
61	figliuola di Bastiano da Vichio	–	Da Viccio	1553	–	1553
62	Lexandra di Bastiano di Benedetto Francesci	Girolama	Franceschi	1554	–	1583
63	Benedetta servigiale	Benedetta	–	1555	–	†1555
64	Agniesa servigiale	Agniesa	–	1555	–	†1555
65	Fioretta di Bernardo Micceri	Fioretta	Micceri	1555	–	1619
66	Lucrezia di Giovanni Compagni	Faustina	Compagni	1555	–	1619
67	Brigida servigiale	Brigida	–	1555	–	1562
68	Lena servigiale	Lena	–	1555	–	1558
69	Argentina dal Raffaelo Guidoni	Argentina	Guidoni	1556	–	1583
70	Aurelia di Domenico Ghiudetti	Aurelia	Giudetti	1557	–	1619
71	Benedetta servigiale	Benedetta	–	1558	–	1558
72	Figliuola di Piero Mariani	Giulia	Mariani	1558	10	†1633
73	Maria di Nicholo Rondinegli	Violante	Rondinelli	1559	–	1619

Table B.1(e) The women of San Matteo, 1560–1580 († death; * *in serbanza/serbo*)

	Name	Religious name	Family name	first recorded	entry age	last recorded
74	Fiametta	Fiammetta	Morelli	1560	–	1583
75	figliuola di Francesco Brava serviglia	–	Brava	1560	–	1560
76	Lodovica di Francesco Vinta	Lodovica	Vinta	1560	–	1619
77	Vittoria di Francesco dastia servigiale	Vittoria	D'Astia	1560	–	1594?
78	Pulisena di Francesco Vinta	Pulisena	Vinta	1561	–	†1633
79	Chiara di Simone Rondinegli	Chiara	Rondinelli	1562	–	†1612
80	Porzia di Giovanni Buonacorsi	Porzia	Buonaccorsi	1562	–	1608
81	Vincentia	Vincenza	Buondelmonte	1562	–	1619
82	Prudentia	Prudenzia	Nenci	1562	–	1583
83	Verginia Canigiani	Virginia	Canigiani	1562	–	†1633
84	Silvia	Silvia	Canigiani	1562	–	1583
85	Ermellina di Gianotto Gianotti	Ermellina	Giannotti	1563	–	1619
86	Laura di Francesco Gaetani	Laura	Gaetani	1563	–	1619
87	Lavinia	Lavinia	–	1572	–	1583
88	figliuola di Raffaello della Vacchia	–	della Vacchia	1578	–	1578
89	figliuola di Taddeo Masini	–	Masini	1578	–	1578
90	Fiammetta di Ser Domenico Buonaccorsi	Deodata	Buonaccorsi	1579	11	1619
91	Isabella Santini	Lucrezia	Santini	1580	11	1635
92	Virginia Santini	Justina	Santini	1580	6	1619

Table B.1(f) The women of San Matteo, 1582–1595 († death; * in serbanza/serbo)

	Name	Religious name	Family name	first recorded	entry age	last recorded
93	Camila di Giovanfranc.o Altoviti	Alexandra	Altoviti	1582	–	1619
94	Francesca di Niccolo della Scala	Francesca	della Scala	1582	–	1582
95	Maria di Jacopo Squadrini	Maria Maddalena	Squadrini	1582	–	1633
96	Francesca di Giovanni Salvetti	Maria Francesca	Salvetti	1582	–	1619
97	Isabella Baroncelli	Isabella	Baroncelli	1583	–	1583
98	Hortensia del Nente	Ortenzia	Nenci	1583	–	1633
99	Smeralda	Smeralda	Panzanini	1583	–	1617
100	Contessa	Contessa	Boscoli	1583	–	1608
101	Dianora	Dianora	–	1583	–	1583
102	Daria	Daria	–	1583	–	1583
103	Laudomina	Laudomina	Squarcialupi	1583	–	†1604
104	Caterina Angiola di Anselmi	Caterina Angela	Anselmi	1583	>14	†1633
105	Clarice Burci	Clarice	Burci	1583	–	1619
106	Emilia de Baldini	Emilia	Baldini	1583	–	1619
107	Ursina del cavachi	Ursina	Cavacchi	1583	–	1619
108	Lessandra di Francesco del Pace	Maria Grazia	del Pace	1586	12	†1633
109	Lisabetta di Francesco Gherardini	Lisabetta	Gherardini	1593	14	1619
110	Vittoria servigiale	Vittoria	–	1594	–	†1594
111	Lisabetta di Jacopo Rossini	Lisabetta	Rossini	1594	–	1594
112	Domenica di Michele Potrini servigiale	Domenica	Potrini	1595	15	1595
113	Lisabetta di Jacopo Orsini servigiale	Lisabetta	Orsini	1595	–	1595

Table B.1(g) The women of San Matteo, 1596–1600 († death; * *in serbanza/serbo*)

	Name	Religious name	Family name	first recorded	entry age	last recorded
114	Nannina di Giovanni Franceschi	Maria Vittoria	Franceschi	1596	13	1619
115	Contessa di Alessandro Fioravati	Cherubina	Floravati	1596	–	1633
116	Dianora di Francesco Ristori	Dianora	Ristori	1596	20	1596
117	Caterina di Agostino Fagioli	Caterina Electa	Fagioli	1597	13	1619
118	Margherita di Benedetto Franceschi	Leonida	Franceschi	1597	20	1619
119	Maria di Luca Antonio Ninci servigiale	Maria (Teodora?)	Ninci	1597	–	1597
120	Gostanza di Nicholo Laschi servigiale	Costanza	Laschi	1597	17	1619
121	Maddalena di Luca Mei	Ippolita	Mei	1598	12	1619
122	Maddalena di Jacopo Gherardi	Argentina	Gherardi	1598	12	1608
123	Luisa di Lionardo Pitti	Luisa	Pitti	1599	16	1644
124	Gostanza di Vincenzio Davanzati	Maria Vincenza	Davanzati	1599	–	1619
125	Cassandra di Marco Attavanti	Maria Giacinta	Attavanti	1600	13	1619
126	Polita da Signa servigiale	Polizia	Da Signa	1600	–	1600
127	Portia di Dino Compagni	Porzia	Compagni	1600	13	1600
128	Livia di Agustino Giani*	Livia	Gianni	1600	14	1600

Table B.1(h) The women of San Matteo, 1601–1602 († death; * in serbanza/serbo)

	Name	Religious name	Family name	first recorded	entry age	last recorded
129	Marietta di Rafaello Cavaresi*	Marietta	Cavaresi	1601	16	1601
130	Maria di Jacopo Squadrini*	Maria	Squadrini	1601	–	1601
131	Lisabetta di Jacopo Squadrini*	Lisabetta	Squadrini	1601	13	1601
132	Francesca di Miggiotto Bardi*	Francesca	Bardi	1601	10	1601
133	Anna di Cino Cini*	Anna	Cini	1601	10	1601
134	Lucrezia di Bernardo Pauli	Lucrezia	Pauli	1601	14	1601
135	Maddalena di Ridolfo Filidolfi da Panzano	Maria Angelica	Filidolfi	1601	13	1619
136	Lessandra di Francesco Rondinelli	Camilla	Rondinelli	1601	12	1633
137	Cassandra di Luca Mei	Cassandra	Mei	1601	9	1619
138	Lucrezia di Antonio Zeffi	Anna	Zeffi	1601	13	1619
139	Maddalena di Domenico Pini servigliale	Maddalena	Pini	1601	18	1601
140	Caterina di Piero Gaetani	Dionisia	Gaetani	1602	12	1619
141	Camilla di Alessandro Chellini*	Camilla	Chellini	1602	8	1602
142	Anna di Alessandro Chellini*	Anna	Chellini	1602	9	1602
143	Aurelia di Baldovino Nucci	Olimpia	Nucci	1602	13	1619
144	Isabella di Luca Castrucci	Maria Virginia	Castrucci	1602	–	1619
145	Maria di Francesco Guardini	Maria Clemenzia	Guardini	1602	13	1619
146	Caterina di Rafaello Cavaresi*	Caterina	Cavaresi	1602	–	1602

Table B.1(i) The women of San Matteo, 1602 cont.–1610 († death; * in serbanza/serbo)

	Name	Religious name	Family name	first recorded	entry age	last recorded
147	Ginevra di Marco Gottavanti*	Ginevra	Gottavanti	1602	10	1602
148	Camilla di Benedetto Giramonte*	Camilla	Giramonti	1602	–	1602
149	Margherita di Simone Morelli*	Margherita	Morelli	1602	10	1602
150	Isabella di Benedetto Giramonti	Isabella	Giramonti	1602	16	1602
151	Silvia di Ercole Squarcialupi	Laudomina	Squarcialupi	1603	12	1619
152	Lessandra di Cino Cini*	Alessandra	Cini	1603	12	1603
153	Laura di Giovanbattista Spicchio	Massimillia	Spicchio	1603	12	1619
154	Francesca di Ruberto Brandolini	Francesca	Brandolini	1603	–	1603
155	Caterina di Alessandro benedetti	Caterina	Benedetti	1604	–	1604
156	Camilla di Girolamo Anselmi	Camilla	Anselmi	1605	8	1619
157	Verginia di Girolamo Anselmi*	Virginia	Anselmi	1605	11	1605
158	Oretta de Buonaccorsi	Oretta	Buonaccorsi	1608	–	1619
159	Nannina della Fonte	Nannina	della Fonte	1608	–	1619
160	Angelica de Canigiani	Angelica	Canigiani	1608	–	1619
161	Isabella de Serdonati	Isabella	Serdonati	1608	–	1619
162	Maria de Naldi	Maria	Naldi	1608	–	1619
163	Caterina di Leonardo Berti	Caterina	Berti	1610	–	1610
164	Giovanetta Anselmi	Maria Benedetta	Anselmi	1610	–	1619

Table B.1(j) The women of San Matteo, 1611–1619 († death; * in serbanza/serbo)

	Name	Religious name	Family name	first recorded	entry age	last recorded
165	Ottavia Squarcialupi	Maria Ottavia	Squarcialupi	1611	–	1619
166	Margerita di Bartolomeo Mancini	Dianora	Mancini	1611	–	1619
167	Lorenza di Francesco Bacci	Maria Laura	Bacci	1611	–	1619
168	Luisa di Francesco Panuzzi*	Luisa	Panuzzi	1611	–	1611
169	Maria di Girolamo Torcitore*	Maria	Torcitore	1612	–	1612
170	Maria di Antonio Archilei	Maria Eletta	Archilei	1612	–	1641
171	Virginia di Galileo Galilei	Maria Celeste	Galilei	1612	–	†1634
172	Livia di Galileo Galilei	Arcangela	Galilei	1612	–	†1658
173	Smeralda Buonacorsi	Maria Leonora	Buonaccorsi	1612	–	1612
174	Alessandro di Ridolfo Filidolfi	Alessandra	Filidolfi	1612	–	1612
175	Caterina di Bastiano Santini*	Caterina	Santini	1618	–	1621
176	Francesca di Camillo Portiani*	Francesca	Portiani	1618	–	1618
177	Caterina di Giovanbattista Baschieri*	Caterina	Baschieri	1618	–	1618
178	Lucrezia di Antonio Pieri*	Lucrezia	Pieri	1618	–	1618
179	Ermellina di Piero Larciani	Ermellina	Larciani	1619	–	1619
180	Francesca di Camillo Posticci	Francesca	Posticci	1619	–	1619
181	Diamante de Bacci	Diamante	Bacci	1619	–	1633
182	Maria Felix della Fonte	Maria Felix	della Fonte	1619	–	1619

Table B.1(k) The women of San Matteo, 1619 cont.–1633 († death; * *in serbanza/serbo*)

	Name	Religious name	Family name	first recorded	entry age	last recorded
183	Beatrix de Canigiani	Beatrix	Canigiani	1619	–	1619
184	Maria Angela de Landi	Maria Angela	Landi	1619	–	1619
185	Francesca de Soldani	Francesca	Soldani	1619	–	1619
186	Maria Anna de Rosselli	Maria Anna	Rosselli	1619	–	1619
187	Maria Gabriella del Legia	Maria Gabriella	del Legia	1619	–	1619
188	Angela de Grassi	Angela	Grassi	1619	–	1619
189	Maria Fides di Bonelli	Maria Fides	Bonelli	1619	–	1619
190	Isabella Landucci	Clara	Landucci	1619	–	1619
191	Maria Lucrezia de Bruni	Maria Lucrezia	Bruni	1619	–	1619
192	Margherita de quarli	Margherita	Quarli	1619	–	1619
193	Egeria di Giulio Corsi*	Giulia?	Corsi	1620	–	1620
194	Prudentia di Giovanni Tani*	Prudentia	Tani	1620	–	1620
195	Francesca di Giovanni Tani*	Francesca	Tani	1620	–	1620
196	Maria di Piermaria della Pozza*	Maria	della Pozza	1620	–	1620
197	Maddalena Ninci	Maddalena	Ninci	1621	–	1621
198	Maria Silvia Boscoli	Maria Silvia	Boscoli	1633	–	†1633

References

Animuccia, Giovanni. 1565. *Il primo libro de madrigali a tre voci*. Rome: Dorico.

Aplin, John. 1979. 'The Survival of Plainsong in Anglican Music: Some Early English Te-Deum Settings'. *Journal of the American Musicological Society* 32 (2): 247–75. https://doi.org/10.2307/831079.

Archdiocese of Florence. 1603. *Decreta dioecesanae Florentinae synodi: celebrata ab Illustriss. ac Reuerendiss. D.D. Alexandro Medice S.R.E. Cardinali & Archiepiscopo Florentino etc.* Florence: Sermartelli.

Aulisio, Giovanni Tommaso, ed. 1595. *Compendium priuilegiorum fratrum minorum et aliorum mendicantium et non mendicantium*. Vol. 2. Naples: Carlino et Pace.

Baggiani, Franco. 1982. 'Musicisti in Pisa: I maestri di Cappella della Primaziale'. *Bollettino storico pisano* 51: 271–94.

Baroffio, Giacomo, and Eun Ju Kim. 2004. *Iam sanctae Clarae claritas: l'ufficio ritmico di santa Chiara nella tradizione arborense*. Milan: Coro dell'Università Cattolica.

Blackburn, Bonnie J. 2015. 'The Lascivious Career of B-Flat'. In *Eroticism in Early Modern Music*, edited by Laurie Stras and Bonnie J. Blackburn, 19–42. Farnham: Ashgate Publishing.

Boccali, P. Giovanni. 2011. *Cum hymnis et canticis. Gaudeat Mater Ecclesia in festo sancte Clare virginis Assisiensis*. Assisi: Edizioni Porziuncola.

Bonechi, Maddalena. 2016. '"Nuove musiche" nella Firenze di primo Seicento: luoghi, occasioni, prassi esecutive, musiche e testi'. PhD, Florence: Università degli Studi.

Borren, Charles van den. 1934. 'Inventaire des manuscrits de musique polyphonique qui se trouvent en Belgique'. *Acta musicologica* 6: 23–29.

Boscolo, Lucia. 1996. 'L'antologia polifonica fiorentina del 1560 nel Codice Bruxelles 27766'. *Rassegna veneta di studi musicali* 11/12: 177–267.

——— 2002. 'Una composizione a 4 voci in notazione quadrata nel codice fiorentino di Bruxelles 27766'. In *Un millennio di polifonia liturgica tra oralità e scrittura*, edited by Giulio Cattin and F. Alberto Gallo, 11–18. Venice: Società Editrice Il Mulino.

Bruning, Fr. Eliseo, ed. 1951. *Cantuale Romano-Seraphicum, editio tertia, aucta ac Rituali necnon Antiphonali Ordinis*. Paris: Desclée & Soc.

Carter, Tim. 2024. 'Ottavio Rinuccini's Narciso: A Study and Edition'. *Journal of Seventeenth-Century Music* 30 (1). https://sscm-jscm.org/jscm-issues/volume-30-no-1/carter-rinuccini-narciso/.

Cattin, Giulio. 2003. 'Le laude del Giubileo (Ms. Bruxelles Cons.27766)'. In *Studi sulla lauda offerti all'autore da F. A. Gallo e F. Luisi*, edited by Patrizia Dalla Vecchia, 439–57. Istituto di Paleografia Musicale–Roma. Serie III: Miscellanea. Rome: Torre d'Orfeo.

Cingoli, Benedetto da. 1503. *Sonecti, barzelle, et capitoli del claro poeta B. Cingulo*. Rome: Johann Besicken.

Cummings, Anthony M. 1981. 'Toward an Interpretation of the Sixteenth-Century Motet'. *Journal of the American Musicological Society* 34 (1): 43–59. https://doi.org/10.2307/831034.

——— 2004. *The Maecenas and the Madrigalist: Patrons, Patronage, and the Origins of the Italian Madrigal*. Philadelphia: American Philosophical Society.

Cusick, Suzanne G. 2009. *Francesca Caccini at the Medici Court: Music and the Circulation of Power*. Chicago: University of Chicago Press.

Cyrus, Cynthia. 1990. 'Polyphonic Borrowings and the Florentine Chanson Reworking, 1475—1515'. PhD, Chapel Hill, NC: University of North Carolina.

D'Accone, Frank A. 1983. 'Singolarità di alcuni aspetti della musica sacra fiorentina del Cinquecento'. In Garfagnini, Gian Carlo (ed.), *Firenze e la Toscana dei Medici nell'Europa del '500*, vol. 2, 513–37. Florence: Leo S. Olschki.

Fabris, Dinko. 2011. 'Galileo and Music: A Family Affair'. In *The Inspiration of Astronomical Phenomena VI. Proceedings of a Conference Held October 18–23, 2009 in Venezia, Italy*, edited by Enrico Corsini, 441: 57–72. San Francisco: Astronomical Society of the Pacific.

Fenlon, Iain, and James Haar. 1988. *The Italian Madrigal in the Early Sixteenth Century: Sources and Interpretation*. Cambridge: Cambridge University Press.

Filippi, Daniele V. 2017. '"Audire missam non est verba missae intelligere...": The Low Mass and the *Motetti missales* in Sforza Milan'. *Journal of the Alamire Foundation* 9 (1): 11–32. https://doi.org/10.1484/J.JAF.5.114048.

Francescani. 1596. *Statuta, constitutiones, et decreta generalia: Familiae Cismontanae ord. S. Franc. de Obseruantia etc.* Piacenza: Giovanni Bazachi.

——— 1713. *Constituzioni del venerabil monastero di S. Matteo in Arcetri militante sotto l'insegne del serafico padre San Francesco etc.* Florence: Guiducci e Franchi.

Galilei, Galileo. 1900. *Le opere di Galileo Galilei. Edizione nazionale, etc.*, edited by Antonio Favaro and Isidoro del Lungo. Vol. 10. Florence: n.p.

——— 1901. *Le opere di Galileo Galilei. Edizione nazionale, etc.*, edited by Antonio Favaro and Isidoro del Lungo. Vol. 11. Florence: n.p.

1902. *Le opere di Galileo Galilei. Edizione nazionale, etc.*, edited by Antonio Favaro and Isidoro del Lungo. Vol. 12. Florence: n.p.

1903. *Le opere di Galileo Galilei. Edizione nazionale, etc.*, edited by Antonio Favaro and Isidoro del Lungo. Vol. 13. Florence: n.p.

1904a. *Le opere di Galileo Galilei. Edizione nazionale, etc.*, edited by Antonio Favaro and Isidoro del Lungo. Vol. 14. Florence: n.p.

1904b. *Le opere di Galileo Galilei. Edizione nazionale, etc.*, edited by Antonio Favaro and Isidoro del Lungo. Vol. 15. Florence: n.p.

1909. *Le opere di Galileo Galilei. Edizione nazionale, etc.*, edited by Antonio Favaro and Isidoro del Lungo. Vol. 20. Florence: n.p.

Galilei, Suor Maria Celeste. 1983. *Lettere al padre*, edited by Giuliana Morandini. Torino: Rosa.

2000. *Sister Maria Celeste's Letters to Her Father, Galileo*, edited and translated by Rinaldina Russell. New York: Writers Club Press.

2001. *Letters to Father: Suor Maria Celeste to Galileo, 1623–1633*, edited and translated by Dava Sobel. New York: Walker & Co.

Gemignani, Marco. 2002. 'The Navies of the Medici: The Florentine Navy and the Navy of the Sacred Military Order of St Stephen, 1547–1648'. In *War at Sea in the Middle Ages and the Renaissance*, edited by John B. Hattendorf and Richard W. Unger, 169–86. Woodbridge: Boydell & Brewer.

Giacomelli, Gabriele. 2001. '"Ecce quam bonum". Una tradizione melodica per canoni e laude, messe e mottetti, salmi e trionfi'. In *Una città e il suo profeta: Firenze di fronte al Savonarola*, edited by Gian Carlo Garfagnini, 319–423. Florence: SISMEL – Edizioni del Galluzzo.

Graca, Daniela. 2024. 'Blood and Milk on Thy Tongue: Suor Domenica da Paradiso's Theology of Divine Love and Vocality in the *Laude* of La Crocetta (c.1515–1553)'. MA, Toronto: McGill University.

Gruppo di lavoro 'Firenze' dell'Università Ca' Foscari di Venezia. 2006. 'La mappa della musica da chiesa a Firenze tra Cattedrale, laudesi e committenza "minore"'. In *Produzione, circolazione e consumo consuetudine e quotidianità della polifonia sacra nelle chiese monastiche e parrocchiali dal tardo Medioevo alla fine degli Antichi Regimi*, edited by David Bryant and Elena Quaranta, 193–226. Quaderni di 'musica e storia' 5. Bologna: Il mulino.

Johnstone, Andrew. 2006. '"High" Clefs in Composition and Performance'. *Early Music* 34 (1): 29–53. https://doi.org/10.1093/em/cah190.

Kirkendale, Warren. 1993. *The Court Musicians in Florence during the Principate of the Medici: With a Reconstruction of the Artistic Establishment*. Florence: L. S. Olschki.

Landucci, Luca. 1883. *Diario fiorentino dal 1450 al 1516*, edited by Jodoco del Badia. Florence: G. C. Sansoni.

Leonardi, Matteo. 2021. *Storia della lauda (secoli XIII–XVI)*. Collection 'Epitome musical'. Turnhout: Brepols.

Lowe, K. J. P. 2003. *Nuns' Chronicles and Convent Culture in Renaissance and Counter-Reformation Italy*. Cambridge: Cambridge University Press.

Macey, Patrick. 1998. *Bonfire Songs: Savonarola's Musical Legacy*. Oxford: Clarendon Press.

——— 2007. 'Filippo Salviati, Caterina de'Ricci, and Serafino Razzi: Patronage Practices for the Lauda and Madrigal at the Convent of S. Vincenzo in Prato'. In *Cappelle musicali fra corte, stato e chiesa nell'Italia del rinascimento*, edited by Franco Piperno, Gabriella Biagi Ravenni, and Andrea Chegai, 349–72. Florence: Olschki.

Milsom, John. 2018. 'The T-Mass: *quis scrutatur?*' *Early Music* 46 (2): 319–31. https://doi.org/10.1093/em/cay019.

——— 2020. 'Attending (to) Masses in the Long 16th Century'. *Early Music* 48 (2): 251–57. https://doi.org/10.1093/em/caaa035.

Newbigin, Nerida. 1983. *Nuovo corpus di sacre rappresentazioni fiorentine del Quattrocento: edite e inedite tratte da manoscritti coevi o ricontrollate su di essi*. Bologna: Commissione per i Testi di Lingua.

Pagnini, Pietro. 1936. 'Alcuni documenti galileiani inediti'. *Atti della Società Colombaria fiorentina* 13: 43–81.

Planchart, Alejandro. 2006. 'The Books that Guillaume Du Fay Left to the Chapel of Saint Stephen'. In *Sine musica nulla disciplina: studi in onore di Giulio Cattin*, 175–212. Padua: Il Poligrafo.

Puliti, A. 1738. *Vita della serva di Dio suor Maria Angiola Gini monaca professa nel monastero di San Matteo in Arcetri . . . .* Florence: Viviani.

Repetti, E. 1845. *Dizionario geografico fisico storico della Toscana – Supplemento*. Florence: n.p.

Ridolfi, Roberto. 1958. 'Diario fiorentino di anonimo delle cose occorse l'anno 1537'. *Archivio storico italiano* 116 (4): 544–70.

Rodin, Jesse. 2012. *Josquin's Rome: Hearing and Composing in the Sistine Chapel*. AMS Studies in Music. New York: Oxford University Press.

Rombough, Julia. 2024. *A Veil of Silence: Women and Sound in Renaissance Italy*. Cambridge, MA: Harvard University Press.

Ryan, Mary Ellen. 2019. '"Our Enemies Are Gathered Together": The Politics of Motets During the Second Florentine Republic, 1527–1530'. *Journal of Musicology* 36 (3): 295–330. https://doi.org/0.1525/jm.2019.36.3.295.

Sand, Alexa. 2014. *Vision, Devotion, and Self-Representation in Late Medieval Art*. Cambridge: Cambridge University Press. https://doi.org/10.1017/CBO9781139424769.

Santoni, Luigi. 1847. *Raccolta di notizie storiche riguardanti le chiese dell'arci-diogesi di Firenze: tratte da diversi autori*. Florence: G. Mazzoni.

Schwartz, Roberta Freund. 2001. 'From *Criado* to Canonization: Music in the Life of St. Francis of Borja'. In *Essays on Music and Culture in Honour of Herbert Kellman*, edited by Barbara Haggh, 193–200. Paris: Minerve.

Spadolini, Giovanni. 1984. 'Il nostro Pian dei Giullari'. *Nuovo antologia* 545: 138–43.

Stras, Laurie. 2012. 'The *Ricreationi per monache* of Suor Annalena Aldobrandini'. *Renaissance Studies* 26 (1): 34–59. https://doi.org/10.1111/j.1477-4658.2011.00789.x.

―――. 2017a. 'The Performance of Polyphony in Early Sixteenth-Century Italian Convents'. *Early Music* 45 (2): 195–214. https://doi.org/10.1093/em/cax023.

―――. 2017b. '*Voci pari* Motets and Convent Polyphony in the 1540s: The *materna lingua* Complex'. *Journal of the American Musicological Society* 70 (3): 617–96. https://doi.org/10.1525/jams.2017.70.3.617.

―――. 2018. *Women and Music in Sixteenth-Century Ferrara*. Cambridge: Cambridge University Press. https://doi.org/10.1017/9781316650455.

―――. 2024. 'A Response to Joshua Rifkin ("Singing Nuns? More on the Story of Verona 761"): ❖ Observation ❖'. *Early Music* 52 (2): 262–71. https://doi.org/10.1093/em/caad034.

Strocchia, Sharon T. 2003. 'Taken into Custody: Girls and Convent Guardianship in Renaissance Florence'. *Renaissance Studies* 17 (2): 177–200. https://doi.org/10.1111/1477-4658.t01-1-00016.

―――. 2009. *Nuns and Nunneries in Renaissance Florence*. Baltimore: Johns Hopkins University Press.

Sutherland, David A. 1972. 'A Second Corteccia Manuscript in the Archives of Santa Maria del Fiore'. *Journal of the American Musicological Society* 25 (1): 79–85. https://doi.org/10.2307/830301.

Varchi, B. 1721. *Storia fiorentina di messer Benedetto Varchi*. Colonia: Pietro Martello.

Verna, Cristiano, and Antonio Zaccaria. 2018. *Il castello di Castrocaro. Storia e tecnica di una terra di confine*. Castrocaro Terme: Cristiano Verna.

Volkhardt, Ulrike. 2009. 'Audivi vocem in celo: Ein (Aufführungs-) Praxisbericht über die Wiederentdeckung und Ersteinspielung von Musikalien aus den Lüneburger Klöstern'. In *Musikort Kloster. Kulturelles Handeln von Frauen in der Frühen Neuzeit*, edited by Susanne Rode-Breymann, 159–66. Cologne: Böhlau Verlag.

Weaver, Elissa. 2002. *Convent Theatre in Early Modern Italy: Spiritual Fun and Learning for Women*. Cambridge: Cambridge University Press.

Wilson, Blake. 1992. *Music and Merchants: The Laudesi Companies of Republican Florence*. Oxford University Press. https://doi.org/10.1093/oso/9780198161769.003.0004.

———. 2001. 'Hora mai sono in età: Savonarola and Music in Laurentian Florence'. In *Una città e il suo profeta: Firenze di fronte al Savonarola*, edited by Gian Carlo Garfagnini, 283–309. Florence: SISMEL – Edizioni del Galluzzo.

———. 2009. *Singing Poetry in Renaissance Florence: The Cantasi Come Tradition (1375–1550)*. Florence: Leo S. Olschki.

Yardley, Anne Bagnall. 1986. '"Full weel she soong the service dyvyne": The Cloistered Musicians in the Middle Ages'. In *Women Making Music: The Western Art Tradition*, edited by Jane Bowers and Judith Tick, 15–38. Urbana: University of Illinois Press.

Acknowledgements

I acknowledge with thanks the support of the Leverhulme Trust for the award of an Emeritus Fellowship to complete this research. My gratitude also to the libraries and archives whose staff have been so unfailingly gracious: in Florence, the Archivio di Stato, the Archivio Storico Arcivescovile, the Biblioteca Nazionale Centrale, the Opera di Santa Maria del Fiore, and the Museo di San Marco; in Rome, the Biblioteca Apostolica Vaticana; in Brussels, the Bibliothèque du Conservatoire Royal. At this last institution, I remain indebted to Olivia Wahnon de Oliveira, Hugo Rodriguez, and Isabelle Mattart for their willingness to answer my regular emails asking about updates on MS 27766's restoration. I am grateful to Marc Busnel for his reproduction of the manuscript seen in the video example. Thanks, too, to the editor of this series, Rhiannon Mathias, and CUP's Kate Brett, for their patience and kind assistance. An earlier version of some of this work appears as 'Music, Community, Family, and Friendship at the Clarissan Convent of San Matteo in Arcetri (1540–1630)', in *Women and Music Networks in Europe*, edited by Ascensión Mazuela Anguita, 77–95 (Granada: University of Granada Press, 2025).

And as ever, eternal thanks to all the wonderful musicians of Musica Secreta, and to Vidda Le Feber, for their contributions to the audiovisual material in this Element. Full versions of several works discussed appear on Musica Secreta's albums *From Darkness Into Light: Antoine Brumel's Complete Lamentations of Jeremiah for Good Friday*. Musica Secreta, Obsidian CD719, 2019 (Audio 1 and 20, used with permission); *Mother, Sister, Daughter*. Musica Secreta, Lucky Music LCKY001, 2022 (Audio 15–17).

All other audio examples are drawn from the companion album to this Element: *Ricordanze: A record of love*. Musica Secreta, Lucky Music LCKY005, 2025.

Cambridge Elements

Women in Music

Rhiannon Mathias
Bangor University

Dr. Rhiannon Mathias is Lecturer and Music Fellow in the School of Music and Media at Bangor University. She is the author of a number of women in music publications, including *Lutyens, Maconchy, Williams and Twentieth-Century British Music: A Blest Trio of Sirens* (2012), and gives frequent conference presentations, public lectures and radio broadcasts on the topic. She is also the editor of the Routledge Handbook on *Women's Work in Music*, a publication which arose from the First International Conference on Women's Work in Music (Bangor University, 2017), which she instigated and directed. The success of the first conference led to her directing a second conference in 2019.

About the Series

Elements in Women in Music provides an exciting and timely resource for an area of music scholarship which is undergoing rapid growth. The subject of music, women and culture is widely researched in the academy, and has also recently become the focus of much public debate in mainstream media.

This international series will bring together many different strands of research on women in classical and popular music. Envisaged as a multimedia digital 'stage' for showcasing new perspectives and writing of the highest quality, the series will make full use of online materials such as music sound links, audio and/or film materials (e.g. performances, interviews – with permission), podcasts and discussion forums relevant to chosen themes.

The series will appeal primarily to music students and scholars, but will also be of interest to music practitioners, industry professionals, educators and the general public.

Cambridge Elements⹀

Women in Music

Elements in the Series

Grażyna Bacewicz, The 'First Lady of Polish Music'
Diana Ambache

Leokadiya Kashperova
Graham Griffiths

Julie Reisserová (1888–1938)
Jean-Paul C. Montagnier

Bandleader Mrs Mary Hamer and Her Boys: Popular Music and Dance Cultures in Interwar Liverpool
Laura Hamer and Michael Brocken

Music at a Florentine Convent: The Biffoli-Sostegni Manuscript and Suor Maria Celeste Galilei
Laurie Stras

A full series listing is available at: www.cambridge.org/EWIM

For EU product safety concerns, contact us at Calle de José Abascal, 56–1º, 28003 Madrid, Spain or eugpsr@cambridge.org.

www.ingramcontent.com/pod-product-compliance
Ingram Content Group UK Ltd.
Pitfield, Milton Keynes, MK11 3LW, UK
UKHW021647190326
469097UK00032B/1315